EARLY INTERVENTIONS IN CHILD ABUSE:

THE ROLE OF THE POLICE OFFICER

by

Joy Dan Graves

Published by
R & E PUBLISHERS
P. O. Box 2008
Saratoga, California 95070

Library of Congress Card Catalog Number
81-85982

I.S.B.N.
0-88247-697

*Dedicated in memory of
my mother,
Fetna Pauline Williams
and my father,
Tom Pryor*

TABLE OF CONTENTS

Page

LIST OF FIGURES

LIST OF TABLES

LIST OF APPENDICES

ACKNOWLEDGEMENTS

I want to express my thanks to the many people who have cooperated with me in the completion of this study. I am truly appreciative for their help and suggestions. My special thanks to Dr. Seymour Zelen for his patience, availability, help and encouragement throughout the project.

I am grateful to the many police officers who contributed their time and energy, and to Chief Daryl Gates for permission to conduct the research. I want to extend special thanks to Commander Stephen M. Downing, Jackie Howell, Barbara Pruitt, and all the investigators in the Abused and Battered Child Unit for their suggestions, cooperation and support throughout the past two years. The staff of the Behavioral Science Services Section; Dr. Martin Reiser, Dr. Susan Saxe, Dr. Nels Klyver, Dr. Bebe Jacobson, Beverly Marrone, Dick Snowden and Dee Murphy; have been supportive and given freely of their time and energy. Thank you.

My thanks to Neal Gross, Ward Mason, And Alexander W. MacEachern, authors of *Explorations in Role Analysis Studies of the School Superintendency Role*, and John Wiley and Sons for their kind permission to use copyrighted material in my study.

I want to express my appreciation to my children, Kathleen, Jeffrey and Gale, and to my grandchildren, Crystal and Brendon, who have been patient, kind and understanding — for their support and encouragement I am truly grateful. And last but not least, I would like to thank my friends for remaining my friends even though my time with them was curtailed.

CHAPTER I

INTRODUCTION

The management of child abuse cases has become a major concern of the public within the last few years. It is interesting that the child abuse syndrome was identified as early as 1874, yet there has been little research done in the area. Most of the research that has been conducted focuses on the child and parents after identification of the syndrome has occurred, and the child and the family have been referred to various agencies established to handle child abuse cases.

There appears to be two divergent views on the involvement of the police in child abuse cases; one states that the police should not be involved at all, and the other states that all child abuse cases or suspected cases be reported to the police. One physician in England has stated, "few aspects in the management of these children generate such heat as the involvement of the police" (Renovoize, 1974, p. 107). In California it is a crime for professionals not to report suspected child abuse to the proper authorities (Penal Code 11161.5), and yet it is estimated that only one-fifth of actual child abuse cases are reported despite the estimate that nearly one million American children are suffering from abuse and neglect at any given time (Younger, 1976, p. 6).

Because child abuse is a crime in every state of the Union

1

and in many other parts of the world, the police have been assigned the initial responsibility for investigating child abuse complaints and arresting child abusers. The Los Angeles Police Department has a special unit that investigates cases of child abuse and makes recommendations for prosecution. The Los Angeles Police Department's position on child abuse cases states:

> This Department supports the judicial system in the handling of child abuse situations. This system properly guarantees the constitutional rights of both the adult and the child. Court intervention is frequently necessary to provide confinement, treatment, and temporary custody for children. Under this system, law enforcement agencies have the responsibility to protect life, preserve property and prevent crime by the proper use of peace officer powers. These powers include emergency entry without warrant and protective custody for victims of abuse. A law enforcement investigator has a thorough knowledge of statutes, case law, and how and where to obtain the necessary legal facts and physical evidence. Police agencies are available to take positive action on a 24 hour basis daily. Mandatory reporting laws requiring that reports be made to police agencies within 36 hours are necessary for the immediate protection of the victim and an adequate case investigation. (L.A.P.D. position paper on child abuse cases, 1979)

Cooperative efforts between the Abused and Battered Child Unit of the Los Angeles Police Department and various community agencies to obtain counseling for the victims of abuse and their families have proven to be inadequate. It appears that a large number of families "get lost in the system" (Howell, 1979) and reconstitute the family into a protective circle that resists outside interventions and perpetuates child abuse. The child is often placed in the position of being the "bad guy" for betraying the family and is coerced into denying any abuse in order to regain status in the family as a trustworthy reliable member. The victim may be severely punished for his betrayal. In sexually abused children, the non-abusing parent or colluding parent may align themselves with the abusing parent and may place the blame on the victim directly or indirectly. Abused children may then view themselves as the perpetrator of the crime rather than the victim.

When the police are called to mediate in a family conflict where the child is the victim of an adult, a crisis situation exists. The literature on crisis intervention (Aguilera, Messick, and Farrel, 1970; Bellak, 1964; Caplan, 1964) suggest that there are certain phases than an individual or family experience in a crisis situation. Initially the family is considered to have been in a state of equilibrium. The child is abused by one or both of the parents. This in itself may not create dis-equilibrium, but when the police are called to mediate in the family conflict, a crisis situation exists. The family moves from a state of equilibrium to one of dis-equilibrium. How soon the family regains a state of equilibrium is dependent on the presence of a number of factors; how the situation is perceived, what type of support is available, and the family's coping mechanisms. Crisis situations tend to resolve themselves after a period of four to six weeks with or without intervention (Caplan, 1964) at which time the family once again achieves a level of equilibrium. This state may be at a lower level, on the same level, or on a higher level than they had functioned at prior to the crisis, depending on the kind of interventions that have been made. A major assumption of this study is that in the initial contact with the police, the abusing parent(s) and the abused child are more open and less defensive because during the crisis situation the child and the adults have not mobilized their defenses during the crisis situation. And, there is a general disoragnization of the personality with a state of dis-equilibrium existing. Likewise, the family as a unit is more disorganized and consequently is more open to reorganization and growth.

Police officers have a unique opportunity to intervene during this state of dis-equilibrium because of their availability on a

24 hour basis, and their legal responsibility for protecting victims. Although police officers have been assigned a specific role in our society which is defined with a set of specifications "for role appropriate behavior" (Preiss and Ehrlich, 1966), the police officer who is assigned to child abuse investigations finds role performance affected by expectations of the abused child, the abusing parent, the non-abusing parent, the siblings, and others in the household. These range from expecting to be arrested to being left without protection. The police officer entering into an investigation of child abuse cases finds that his role has been defined by the public through legislation and laws, the judiciary system, the medical community, the Department of Public Social Services, and the police department itself. Yet, the officer is to use his or her own judgment about taking the child into custody, arresting the parents, removing the siblings, leaving the children in the home with the parents and requiring counseling, admonishing the parents for their behavior, becoming involved in some type of follow-up, or any combination.

Bard (1975) has suggested that the collaboration between the social scientist (researcher) and the practitioner (police officer) can provide a rich source of data about human behavior. Naturalistic field studies can enhance the lives of those participating in the study and provide information that will benefit future practitioners (p. 129). The author has been unable to locate any field research in the area of initial police calls involving child abuse complaints or in any area of family violence.

Statement of the Problem

The focus of this study will be on the initial police response to child abuse complaints and will consist of analyses of case studies of the legal, official, and psychological interactions between police officer, the abused or battered child, the family, and other significant people. From the data collected, methods of intervention in family disputes where a child has been abused by an adult will be developed, and relevant methods of training police officers proposed.

Although abuse is defined as any crime against children including physical assault and corporal punishment, physical and emotional assault, emotional deprivation and physical neglect, and sexual exploitation by an adult who is living in the same residence as the child, this study will be limited to physical and sexual abuse. It will be further limited to those child abuse cases reported by the school, the family, the Department of Public Social Services, a neighbor, and investigated by the police at school or in the home.

CHAPTER II

REVIEW OF THE LITERATURE

Because of the inherent belief in the autonomy of the family unit and the controversy over what constitute children's rights and what are parent's rights, the phenomenon of child abuse investigation is relatively new. The subject is the source of a rigorous debate between the civil authorities and the public (Newberger and Bourne, 1978). Although the public would like to believe that the home is a sacred place which is safe from the probing eyes of the public, children represent the home for the future and are now becoming a major resource to be protected through legal intervention. Parents are given the responsibility to raise their children to respect the laws of society and to become productive members of society when they reach their majority. How this is accomplished has been delegated to the parents, and even now when child abuse is coming out of the closet and being discussed in the media, there is still a fine line drawn between discipline and abuse. Gross abuse where the child is physically beaten to death is not debatable, but the question arises when Johnny does something bad and is punished by being beaten with a belt or burned with a cigarette to teach him a lesson. It has been estimated that between 84 to 97% of all parents use some form of physical punishment on their children (Gelles, 1978), and the courts state that parents may

6

punish their children within the bounds of moderation. When punishment inflicts bodily harm and endangers the child's life, the state intervenes through the police and courts (Collins, 1974). A discrepancy exists in opinions of law enforcement officers as to the advisability of having the child who has been abused remain in the home. Mounsey (1975) states "no child should be returned to a home where violence has occurred" (p. 127), and others feel that removal of the child from the home may not be necessary as long as supervision of the abused child is maintained by a public agency (Derdeyn, 1977; Howell, 1979; Pitcher, 1972).

Children were viewed as chattel prior to 1970 (Derdeyn, 1977) and old Roman law stated that the father owns his children and has total control over them (Collins, 1974). In the history of the United States the rights of biological parents to control their children has predominated in the courts and society. The father had rights early in the history of the United States with a gradual shift toward the biological mother having the rights (Derdeyn, 1977). "The Tenth Amendment reserves to the state the area of family domestic relations law" (Derdeyn, 1977, p. 379); however, more and more decisions are being affected by Supreme Court decisions on the Fourteenth Amendment where individual liberty and family privacy are an area of concern (Derdeyn, 1977). These decisions will undoubtedly affect the parents as child care providers.

The family has been viewed as the very cornerstone of American life and removal of the child from his home is a truly momentous decision. This needs to be recognized as a critical moment in the child's life (Derdeyn, 1977), and this decision often is made by the police officer who responds to a child abuse call. The officer is cognizant that the courts may reverse the decision by releasing the child back into the home. Parents' rights to make decisions affecting their children have been upheld in the courts, and it is only recently that some dissenting opinions have been voiced (Derdeyn, 1977). Though interest is being expressed regarding the child's rights, there is also concern that this will interfere with the family and may in fact be contrary to the welfare of the child (Strauss, Gelles, and Steinmetz, 1976).

7

The role of the police involves four functions: identification, receipt of reports, emergency intervention and investigation (United States Department of Health, Education and Welfare, 1977). The reasoning behind law enforcement reporting guides in the model law of the Children's Bureau is that this enforcement agency is the only chain of services which is sure to exist in each community (Paulsen, 1974). Leonski (1975) suggests that there is some question regarding the reasonableness of uniformed police officers making the decision to remove children from their homes in cases of child abuse. He suggests that social workers assisted by police officers should make the decision as to whether or not to remove the child from the home. Collie (1975) states that the police have the means to investigate and clear parents of charges as well as to arrest them, and he further states that the law is for the protection of society and not merely for punishment (p. 124), and Howell (1979) says experience proves that police officers more often do not remove the child from the home but instead place the child in the custody of the parents under the supervision of the Department of Public Social Services and the court. Paulsen (1974) states that the controversy over whether or not the police are adequately trained is secondary to the scarcity of trained workers and economic considerations in utilizing social workers in the policing of parents.

Collins (1974) believes that child abuse should be reported to the police because the police have 24 hours responsibility, people seek help from the police, investigation is one of the police's primary functions, and they are equipped to handle cases. They have legal authority to enter homes on reasonable grounds, they provide a central reporting of cases, and police involvement mandates participation in programs of rehabilitation.

The legal and medical communities have joined forces in formulating a set of social responses of child abuse and have designed legislation and treatment in order to protect the victim and the siblings (Helfer and Kempe, 1974). In spite of the guidelines there are no hard and set rules to follow, and the decision as to whether child abuse, child neglect, or parental discipline

8

of the child has occurred is left to the discretion of the investigator, whether it be medical doctor, nurse, social worker, psychologist, or police officer. An act of violence against the child may be carried out with the consent of the community as in the case of circumcision (Gelles, 1976) or even a tonsillectomy. In child abuse cases lawyers demand evidence, physicians and social workers go on feelings, and the police officer is often caught in the middle. The police officer experiences the need to supply evidence to the lawyer and the courts and also the immediate overwhelming demand to react to the needs of the child and the parents. The police officer is often the first contact the family has with an authority figure appointed by the public to maintain law and order in the community and to protect the rights of the individual (child and parent).

Martin (1976) states that the legal profession, including police officers, has little knowledge of the normal development of a child, and when someone is trained, it is the exception rather than the rule. Collie (1974) indicates that young police officers are not given any special training in how to investigate child abuse cases. The police department assumes that the older officer is reasonably well informed on the subject and will assist the young officer in learning. There is no discussion about how that knowledge is obtained, but the implication is that it occurs through experience. Each police officer is autonomous in the cases he or she investigates and most police officers believe in law and order and in self-control (Renvoize, 1974). These attitudes could lead to insensitivity to the abusing parents and hostility may result when their cooperation is lacking.

Police officer recruits in the Los Angeles Police Department are given a three hour lecture on how to investigate a child abuse case with emphasis on collecting the needed information for conviction and prosecution (Howell, 1979). Likewise, medical personnel are oriented toward diagnosis and delivery of medical services; little attention is given to the psychological needs of the child (Martin, 1976).

The Department of Health, Education and Welfare reports more than one million children are "abused" every year. More

9

than 2,000 die each year from child abuse or neglect. It is worth noting that between 25 and 28% of abusive incidents involve children between the ages of 12 and 18 (Delinquency Rehabilitation Report, 1976), which allows more than simple physical evidence to be obtained (a chronology of events, for example). Although there have been no studies in the literature indicating a correlation between physical abuse and sexual abuse (Martin, 1976), this would be an interesting area to explore. It would also be worth exploring how much of the adolescent child abuse is "purely" sexual abuse.

Summary

There is a dearth of literature on the role of the police officer in child abuse cases. What is available focuses on whether or not the police should be involved. The role of various other professionals has been more clearly delineated while the role of the police officer remains obscure. Since 1970 the public has charged the police with the responsibility of intervention in child abuse cases but has not provided any guidance as to how the officer who responds to a child abuse complaint should intervene. In order to meet this need, it is becoming clear that more research is needed in the area of the initial police call in child abuse complaints. "Little attention in the literature is focused on empirical data collected at the time of abuse" (Strauss, Gelles, and Steinmetz, 1976). The perception of the child, the police officer, and the family of what has happened is paramount if additional training programs for police officers are to be developed.

Literature discussing police officers often utilizes the language of role theory. The role of the policeman is a common phrase in the literature (Bard, 1975; Barocus, 1973; Dean, 1975; Reiser, 1973; and others) and in the public domain. However, the commonality breaks down when behaviors are attached. Dean (1975) states "defining the role of the policeman reminds one of the art of grafting of fruit trees. Branches of various fruit can be grafted onto the trunk of still another kind of fruit. The end product of the grafted branches is unlike the end product of either part before the graft" (p. 186). Biddle and Thomas (1966) have defined role as "a behavioral repertoire characteristic of a person or a position" (p. 11), and a set of standards, descriptions, norms or concepts held by a person or a position (Biddle and Thomas, 1966, p. 11). Dean (1975) states that the police officer's role has changed over the years through the addition of new responsibilities and a change of focus of the officer. More and more the officer is expected to assume the role of mental health worker with little training. Specialization of role is also adding to the complexity of the situation. Reiser (1973) states that "the policeman's role is multiplex" (p. 3), and Preiss and Ehrlich (1966) discuss the process of the recruit taking the role of the police officer, and concluded that the role of the police officer is lacking in clarity and precision when viewed from the various audiences of the Central State Police. . .we found that comparisons within and among rank groups in the department failed to yield appreciable role consensus" (p. 162). In addition they found that the "low order of consensus on role definition or specific expectations may provide considerable flexibility for individual style in role performance. Clearly this line of reasoning needs more focused empirical investigation" (p. 162).

Police officers function in a social setting where there is a set of expectations that are prescribed by the public and include "several main dimensions: peace-keeping, public service, law enforcement and crime suppression and prevention" (Reiser, 1973, p.4). Therefore, role theory provides a theoretical base that is appropriate for the study of police officers investigating child abuse complaints.

Although it is assumed that police officers act in crisis situations regularly, there are few field studies involving police officers as crisis workers in the literature. Auerbach and Kilmann (1977) reviewed crisis intervention literature and did not discuss the role of the police officer in crisis situations. Outcome studies are scarce in psychological literature, and it seems that crisis intervention theory is the least studied form of therapy. Perhaps this is because of the vague nature of crisis intervention theory which has a vague body of knowledge (Auerbach and Kilmann, 1977). Perhaps it also may be a function of the crisis intervention process, which often ends in a referral for further therapy.

Theoretical Framework

Gross, Mason, and MacEachern (1966) examined roles on the basis of a systems model. They proposed the use of a dyad model when the purpose of the investigation is to examine the role in relationship to only one other position as illustrated in Figure 1.

This dyad model can be expanded into a complex systems model as shown in Figure 2 with the focal position being central and various spokes representing counter positions. Gross, Mason, and MacEachern (1966) looked at their data on two levels: (1) the macroscopic, and (2) the microscopic. The macroscopic framework is defined as consensus among all the school super- intendents in Massachusetts and all the school board members in Massachusetts. The subjects of the microscopic framework involved members of small groups composed of a superintendent and his school board or just the members of a single school board.

In this study the author expanded the dyad model into a complex systems model with the police officer occupying the focal position, the siblings occupying counter position 1, the abused child occupying counter position 2, the abusing parent occupying counter position 3, and the non-abusing parent occupying counter position 4. The police officer enters into the family's domain thereby crossing the boundary between home and community. The officer represents the legal community including the police department and the judiciary system. In addition, the officer is the intermediary between the family, the medical community and public social services as illustrated in Figure 3.

This study will be limited to the interaction of the police officers, the abused child, the siblings, the abusing parent, the non-abusing parent, and others involved in the initial investigation

Counter Position

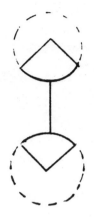

Focal Position

Figure 1. A Dyad Model (Gross, Mason and MacEachern, 1966)

13

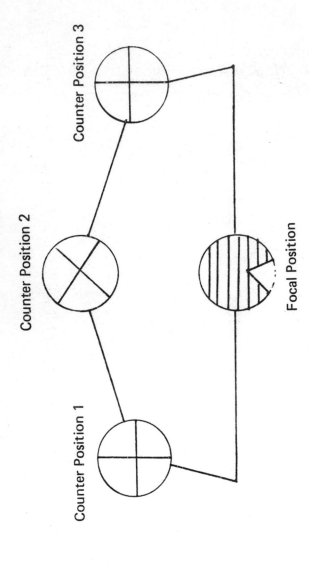

Counter Position 1

Counter Position 2

Counter Position 3

Focal Position

Figure 2. A Systems Model (Gross, Mason and MacEachern, 1966)

14

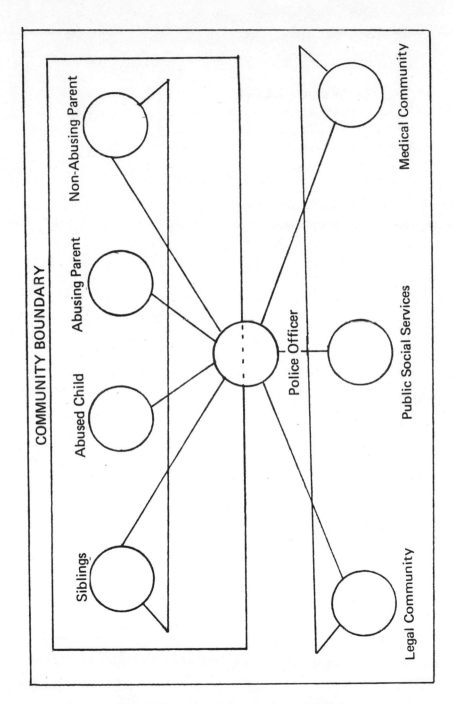

Figure 3. A Complex Systems Model

of a child abuse complaint.

CHAPTER III

METHOD

Research Design

The research design utilized both a descriptive naturalistic field study format in which the researcher accompanied police officers investigating child abuse complaints and an empirical, comparative and correlational aspect. The study was conducted in the Los Angeles Police Department where the researcher was attached to the Behavioral Science Services Section.

Data Collection

Two main approaches to data collection were utilized: (1) ten cases were observed while accompanying police officers in their police cars sent by the Abused and Battered Child Unit of the department to investigate child abuse complaints; (2) the second part consisted of asking (a) 108 field officers to complete a questionnaire that measured attitudes toward rigidity, social responsibility, dogmatism, authoritarianism, compulsivity, and child abuse, as well as (b) securing responses along these same dimensions from 116 police academy recruits.

From consultation with officers assigned to Abused and Battered Child Unit, it was decided that the information developed when accompanying officers in the field who were handling these kinds of investigations, could be utilized to develop a training program for recruits at the police academy.

The researcher also developed a self-administered questionnaire utilizing items from the Rigidity Scale (Rehfisch, 1958), Social Responsibility Scale (Berkowitz and Lutterman, 1968), Four Item F-Scale (Lane, 1955), Short Dogmatism Scale (Schulze, 1962), the literature on child abuse, and from personal communications with police officers investigating child abuse complaints.

A preliminary study was conducted in order to test the mechanics of the questionnaire and to identify trends.

Pilot Study

The pilot study included eight male field police officers from the Garden Grove Police Department who volunteered to be subjects in the study. Four of the eight officers had been with the police department for five to ten years, and four had been with the police department for more than ten years.

All eight of the officers had been to college, two had baccalaureate degrees in criminal justice, three had associate of arts degrees in police science. None of the eight officers was currently enrolled in courses related to child development or family psychology.

There was one single officer and seven married officers of which three were in their first marriage and four had been divorced and had remarried. Data was coded in order to protect the anonymity of the officers participating in the study. One of the officers had five children, three had three to four children, three had one to two children, and one single officer had no children. A summary of the demographic data of the eight police officers in the pilot study appears in Table 1.

Table 1

Pilot Study
Demographic Data of Eight Police Officers from
the Garden Grove Police Department

Subject	Age	Sex	Marital Status	Number of Children**	Years of Police Experience**	Years of College
1	50+	M	DRM*	5	10+	1
2	35-49	M	DRM*	1-2	10+	3
3	23-34	M	M	1-2	10+	2
4	23-34	M	DRM*	1-2	5-10	2
5	35-49	M	M	3-4	10+	2
6	23-34	M	M	3-4	5-10	4
7	23-34	M	DRM*	3-4	5-10	3
8	23-34	M	S	0	5-10	4

N = 8

*Divorced and remarried
**Data coded to condense single categories and preserve individual anonymity.

Although there were no correlations that were statistically significant, several correlations were of interest considering the small sample size. The correlation between Information on Child Abuse and Anxiety and Constraint was .64; the correlation between Personal Racial Attitudes and Dogmatism was .58; and the correlation between Information on Child Abuse and Personal Racial Attitudes was .34. There was a negative correlation of -.43 between Social Racial Attitudes and Anxiety and Constraint. A summary of the results appears in Table 2. While none of the correlations was statistically significant because of the small sample size, some meaningful trends were identified. Since this was a pilot study, the results justified the administration of the questionnaire to a larger sample.

Three scales, Information about Child Abuse, Social Racial Attitudes, and Personal Racial Attitudes were subject to additional statistical analyses and are reported in Table 3. The correlations between Information about Child Abuse, Personal Racial Atti-

Table 2

Intercorrelation Matrix of Social Racial Attitudes, Personal Racial Attitudes, Attitudes Toward Child Abuse Authoritarianism, Dogmatism, Social Responsibility, and Rigidity*

	Social Racial Attitudes	Personal Racial Attitudes	Attitudes Toward Child Abuse	Social Responsibility	Constraints and Conservatism	Perservative Thinking	Anxiety and Constraint	Compulsive Doubting	Rigidity	Authoritarianism	Dogmatism
	1	2	3	4	5	6	7	8	9	10	11
1	-	.04	-.62	.05	.05	.22	-.43	-.37	.08	.10	.10
2			.34	-.33	.33	.46	-.5	.36	-.60	.22	.58
3				-.34	.3	.36	.64	.22	.19	.32	-.14
4					.26	.15	.83	.03	.01	-.52	-.3
5						.11	-.4	.24	.37	.19	.23
6							-.52	-.33	.25	.36	.16
7								.32	.35	-.58	.12
8									.01	-.5	.31
9										.01	.4
10											-.25
11											

N = 8

*None of these correlations was statistically significant likely because of the small sample size.

20

Table 3

Correlations Between Attitudes Toward Child Abuse, Social Racial
Attitudes, and Personal Racial Attitudes

Attitudes Toward Child Abuse and Social Racial Attitudes	Attitudes Toward Child Abuse and Personal Racial Attitudes	Racial Attitudes: Social and Racial
$r_{13} = -.62$	$r_{23} = .343$	$r_{12} = .041$

tudes, and Social Racial Attitudes were not significant statistically, but they indicated a trend that justified additional analyses.

In an effort to identify how these three variables — Social Racial Attitudes, Personal Racial Attitudes, and Information about Child Abuse — influence each other, partial correlations were done and are reported in Table 4. The results of the partial correlations indicated that when Information About Child Abuse items were partialled out, the correlations between Social Racial Attitudes and Personal Racial Attitudes increased from .056 (r_{12}) to .365 ($r_{12.3}$), and when the Social Racial Attitudes were partialled out, the correlation between Information About Child Abuse and Personal Racial Attitudes increased from .343 (r_{23}) to .482 ($r_{23.1}$). When the Personal Racial Attitudes were partialled out, the correlation between Social Racial Attitudes and Information About Child Abuse were changed from -.62 (r_{13}) to -.682 ($r_{13.2}$).

As a result of the pilot study, some changes were made in the questionnaire. For example, the Rehfisch (1958) Rigidity Scale measures compulsivity with two items related to impulsivity. Fass and Zelen developed a CSB-1 Scale that measures compulsivity and orderliness. Fass (1976) administered the scale to college students and validated it with the Ai3Q, a test developed

Partial Correlations Between Attitudes Toward Child Abuse,
Social Racial Attitudes, and Personal Racial Attitudes*

Before Partialling Out	After Partialling Out
$r_{12} = .056$	$r_{12.3} = .365$
$r_{13} = -.62$	$r_{13.2} = .682$
$r_{23} = .343$	$r_{23.1} = .482$

N = 8

*While the result of the partial correlations were gratifying and led to further heuristic thinking, the small size of the sample precluded any interpretation of an acceptable significance level.

by Paul Kline (1971) to measure the obsessional character. She identified two factors: "Factor I was a measure of the opposite of Compusivity" (p. 57) and Factor II dealt with "compulsive characteristics particularly orderliness" (p. 57).

Eight items from the CSB-1 Scale were modified and added to the Child Abuse Questionnaire in order to look at compulsive behaviors related to orderliness and the opposite of compulsivity.

After police department administrative review, items related to racial issues were deleted from the questionnaire. At the suggestion of officers attached to the Juvenile Division, additional child abuse information items were incorporated into the questionnaire.

Hypotheses

The following hypotheses were formulated derived from the literature:

Hypothesis 1: That scores on the Rigidity Scale (Rehfisch, 1958) will be negatively correlated with information police officers have about child abuse; i.e., the higher the rigidity score the higher the child abuse score. This would mean that highly rigid police officers have inadequate information about child abuse issues.

Hypothesis 2: That scores on the Social Responsibility Scale (Berkowitz and Lutterman, 1968) will be positively correlated with the police officer's information about child abuse. This would mean that officers with a sense of social responsibility will be better informed about issues related to child abuse than officers who are lacking in social responsibility.

Hypothesis 3: That scores on the Rigidity Scale (Rehfisch, 1958), Social Responsibility Scale (Berkowitz and Lutterman, 1968), CSB-1 Scale (Fass and Zelen, 1973), Four Item F Scale (Lane, 1955) and Short Dogmatism Scale (Schulze, 1962) will be positively correlated with each other, and that a multiple correlation of these scales will prove to be significant.

Hypothesis 4: No significant difference will exist between the scores of recruits at the police academy and experienced police officers.

Composition of the Questionnaire

There are six scales on the questionnaire; the Child Abuse Information Scale, Rigidity Scale (Rehfisch, 1958), Short Dogmatism Scale (Schulze, 1962), Four Item F Scale (Lane, 1955), CSB-1 Scale (Fass, 1976), and Social Responsibility Scale (Berkowitz and Lutterman, 1968).

Child Abuse Information Scale

The Child Abuse Information Scale includes five subscales; information about the Abusing Parent, Abused Child, Personal History of the Police Officer, Role of the Police Officer, and General Information about child abuse. The development of the Child Abuse Information Scale resulted from reviewing the literature, interviewing officers knowledgeable in the field of child

23

abuse investigations, observing police officers who were trained in child abuse investigations, observing police officers in the field who did not have special training in child abuse investigation, attending classes at the Police Academy relating to child abuse, and consultation with my chairman, Seymour Zelen, Ph.D., an expert in the field with more than 30 years experience exploring child abuse issues.

The literature on child abuse states that it is unusual to find police officers in the field who are knowledgeable about child growth and development (Martin, 1976) and parenting skills. Yet police officers are required to differentiate between abuse, neglect, and discipline. Questions to assess the police officer's level of knowledge about child abuse were constructed and incorporated into the Child Abuse Information Scale. These are:

Parents who abuse their children are often abused as children. (2)

Children two years of age and younger should never be corporally punished. (1)

Neglect is more damaging than physical abuse. (5)

Corporal punishment is necessary in order to maintain order. (5)

Your primary role as a police officer responding to a child abuse complaint is protection of the child. (4)

Sexual abuse of children is worse than physical abuse. (1)

Child abuse in the city is increasing. (5)

Substance abuse parents are more likely to abuse their children than non-substance abusers. (2)

I have witnessed a brother, sister or cousin of mine being

abused by their parents. (3)

Children just don't know what's good for them. (5)

The punishment I received as a child was very harsh. (3)

Present training in child abuse investigation is inadequate. (4)

During the course of disciplining children, bruises are inevitable. (5)

Police officers should be required to complete certain college courses related to families. (4)

Affluent people physically abuse their children less than poor people. (2)

The physical punishment children in my family receive is very harsh. (3)

It is more important to arrest the parent in a child abuse case than to remove the child. (4)

A person who assaults a child should be handled differently than one who assaults an adult. (4)

Harsh physical discipline is that which requires hospitalization. (5)

The best form of discipline is physical punishment. (5)

Misdemeanor child abuse is as bad as felony child abuse. (5)

I find child abuse investigations difficult. (4)

The public has a right to pass judgment on the way the

police handle child abuse cases. (5)

Physical abuse of children is worse than sexual abuse. (1)

As a police officer I have the right to take any action necessary to enforce child abuse laws. (4)

Corporal punishment is the most effective method of disciplining children. (5)

Most parents are very cooperative in the investigation of child abuse cases. (2)

It is easier for me to accept physical abuse of children than it is for me to accept sexual abuse of children. (1)

Please complete this sentence:
Child abuse investigations _____

_____

(1) = Information About Abused Child
(2) = Information About Abusing Parents
(3) = Personal History
(4) = Role of Police Officer
(5) = General Information

Kempe and Helfer (1972) and others state in the literature that abusing parents were often abused children. Police officers come from varied backgrounds, and their personal experience affects the way they handle child abuse investigations. If the discipline they received as children was viewed as harsh or the discipline children in their families receive was seen as harsh, it may affect their decisions in child abuse investigations; therefore, questions designed to elicit this information were incorporated into the questionnaire.

Police officers are responsible for maintaining law and order in the community and are bound by a set of prescribed behaviors.

New recruits model themselves after more experienced officers that they admire (Preiss and Ehrlich, 1966). How individual police officers view that role in child abuse investigations was an area of interest in this study. Questions related to this issue were formulated by interviewing juvenile officers with special training in child abuse investigations, through the observations of experienced officers investigating child abuse complaints, and from the literature. These questions are included in the Child Abuse Information Scale.

Because child abuse is a national phenomenon, there is a general body of knowledge about child abuse issues that police officers need in order to effectively intervene in child abuse cases. The researcher incorporated questions developed through reviewing the literature utilizing information presented by Schneider, Helfer and Pollock (1972) in their predictive questionnaire, Kempe and Helfer (1972), and others.

Rigidity Scale

The Rigidity Scale was developed by Rehfisch in 1958 in order to measure personality rigidity. Rigidity is "characterized by the following qualities: (a) constriction and inhibition, (b) conservatism, (c) intolerance of disorder and ambiguity, (d) observational and perserverative tendencies, (e) social introversion, (f) anxiety and guilt" (Robinson and Shaver, 1973, p. 388). The Rigidity Scale was tested on 60 Air Force captains in order to determine reliability. The test averaged .71 (Robinson and Shaver, 1973, p. 389). On this basis the scale was incorporated into the questionnaire. Responses were changed from True-False to Strongly Agree, Agree, Disagree and Strongly Disagree. High scores reflect high rigidity (see appendix).

Dogmatism Scale

Robinson and Shaver (1973) suggested that additional research needed to be done to see how these items (rigidity) relate to dogmatism and authoritarianism. Therefore, both of these scales were incorporated into the questionnaire.

Schulze (1962) shortened Rokeach's Dogmatism Scale in order to encourage its use in surveys. Reliability on the scale was .66 when cross validated. Robinson and Shaver (1973) suggest that additional research needs to be done in order to see how the Short Dogmatism Scale relates to anxiety and other relevant variables. The construction of the Child Abuse Questionnaire has offered the opportunity to explore the relationship of dogmatism and anxiety as well as other relevant variables such as authoritarianism. Items on the scale were modified to first person, and responses changed from agree a little, agree on the whole, disagree very much, to strongly agree, agree, disagree, and strongly disagree in order to conform to the other measures. Scoring was 1, 2, 4 and 5 with high scores reflecting high degrees of dogmatism. Items are listed in appendices.

F Scale

Four items from the F Scale were selected to include in the questionnaire in order to examine the relationship between authoritarianism, rigidity, dogmatism, socially responsible attitudes, compulsivity, and information about child abuse. Lane (1955) tested these four items on 585 randomly selected adults and found that the four "item Guttman scale yielded a coefficient of reproducibility of 90.4" (Robinson and Shaver, 1973, p. 350). The items were changed to first person, and responses were changed to strongly agree, agree, disagree, and strongly disagree. Lane (1955) used agree, agree quite a bit, agree a little, and disagree. Scoring was 1, 2, 4 and 5 with high scores reflecting high levels of authoritarianism. These are listed in the appendices.

CSB-1 Scale

The CSB-1 Scale was developed by Fass and Zelen (Fass, 1976) and validated with Kline's Ai3Q, a test designed to measure the obsessional character. The correlation on high achieving Cal Tech undergraduates was +.50 indicating that both tests were

affect the police officer's disposition of the complaint?

4. Is it possible to identify recurring themes and phrases in the interaction of police officers and family members in the investigation of child abuse complaints?

5. Who reports child abuse cases, and what are their interactions with the police and the abusing family during the initial call?

6. How do police officers interact with neighbors in complaints concerning possible child abuse?

7. How does police intervention affect abuse patterns in the family?

These questions are incorporated in the interview schedule (see appendices).

Case Studies

Ten child abuse complaint cases were included in the study. Cases were selected on the basis of the first call that came into the Abused and Battered Child Unit where officers responded by going to the home or to the school to investigate the complaint were included in the study; the assumption being that randomization would occur if there was no selection process by the researcher. Each police call was recorded beginning with the initial contact and continuing through the initial investigation and disposition of the case.

In addition to the personal data collected directly from the officer, the researcher also elicited information regarding their reasons for choosing their present assignment; i.e., juvenile officer, training officer, or patrol officer.

In the majority of child abuse complaints, two officers are dispatched to investigate the complaint, and they often separate members of the family during the investigation; one officer talks to the abused child while a second officer is involved with the other family members. The researcher handled this by alternating between the two interactions. In one investigation the researcher went with the abused child and in the next call went with the family.

The researcher defined each officer to a major role based on the interaction of the officer with the family. The *adversary role* was defined as being in opposition to the members of the family involved in child abuse complaint investigation. The *facilitator role* was defined as being helpful to the members of the family involved in child abuse complaint investigations. The *investigator role* was defined as being concerned with uncovering facts to determine whether child abuse had occurred. The *observer role* was defined as paying special attention to events and monitoring what was happening.

The affect of the interactions were evaluative and related primarily to the quality of the interaction. Unsatisfactory affect was defined as lacking in empathy, concern, and understanding while excellent affect was the opposite.

Decision making is a major component of the police officer role. After decisions were made by the police officers the observer asked officers how they made their decision and what criteria they used. Decision making was then categorized as based on the criminal justice code or personal judgment related to cultural context, home appearance, socioeconomic status, expert's opinion and other personal data.

The observer rated the decision making approach as rigid or flexible utilizing a Likert scale of 1 to 100 with 1 being rigid and 100 being flexible. The objective-subjective criteria was rated in the same manner with 1 being subjective and 100 being objective.

Crisis situations resolve themselves in a period of 6 to 8 weeks. The family may function at a lower level or higher level depending on the interaction made. Therefore, a follow-up investigation of the 10 cases included in the sample was conducted by the researcher 6 weeks after the initial investigation. Data was collected through personal contact, telephone contact, and/or from records maintained by the police department. The researcher determined the status of the family at the end of six weeks. The areas examined included: (1) evidence of further abuse, (2) the method of support instituted, (3) was the family being followed, (4) if yes, by whom, (5) was the abusing parent in the family home, (6) if not, where was the abusing parent, (7) was the abused child in the home, and (8) were the siblings in the home. See appendices for interview schedule.

Statistical Analyses

Statistical techniques including analysis of variance, multiple regression, correlation coefficients, t-test for significance of the difference of the means, and descriptive statistical techniques, mean and standard deviation were used to analyze the data from the questions, and the analysis was done on a computer using the *Statistical Package for the Social Sciences* (1975).

Experimental Design

The focus of this study was to explore what police officers do in child abuse investigations and to determine how their attitudes on rigidity, dogmatism, authoritarianism, compulsivity, social responsibility, and so forth related to their knowledge of child abuse and consequently their decision making in child abuse situations. Therefore, two major approaches to the study of the police officer's role in child abuse investigations were used in this field study: (1) an exploratory case study approach looked at what happened in the field when police officers investigate child abuse complaints, and (2) the administration of a questionnaire designed to examine relationships between police officer's attitudes toward rigidity, dogmatism, authoritarianism, compulsivity, social responsibility and levels of information regarding child abuse. Police officer recruits at the Los Angeles Police Department Academy were then compared to experienced police officers employed by the Los Angeles Police Department.

CHAPTER FOOTNOTES

[1]Panel of experts consisted of Zeymour Zelen, Ph.D.; Jackie Howell, officer in charge of the Abused and Battered Child Unit; Barbara Pruitt, officer in charge of Research in the Juvenile Division; a panel of doctoral candidates at CSPP doing research in child abuse, T. Kaleita, M. Mitchell, L. Stone, and L. Tucker; dissertation committee members, A. Urmer, Ph.D., S. Saxe, Ph.D., and M. Reiser, Ed.D.

CHAPTER IV

RESULTS OF THE TEN CASE STUDIES

As a result of the review of the literature, the researcher designed and conducted a descriptive study done in the field with police officers investigating child abuse complaints. The information gathered and reported in this chapter is presented in two sections. The first section focuses on the general characteristics of the child abuse case studies, and the second section focuses on the characteristics of the police officers involved in the investigation. The results are discussed in Chapter VI.

General Characteristics of the Sample of Ten Case Studies Being Investigated by the Police Officers

Ten child abuse complaint cases (Table 5) were included in the study. The researcher accompanied patrol officers on their initial investigation of child abuse complaints. The first call that came into the child abuse unit requiring an officer's response to the home or school to investigate a child abuse complaint was included in the sample. When the case was completed and the disposition made, the researcher returned to the unit and included

Table 5

Summary of the General Characteristics of the Ten Case Studies

Case	Age of Child	Sex of Child	Type of Abuse	Abusing Parent	Ethnic Group	Reporting Party	Disposition of Case
1	5	F	Physical	Mother	White	Neighbor	No report
2	3	M	Physical	Mother	Iranian	School Director	Injury Report
3	10	M	Physical	Father	Black	School Principal	Removal of child and siblings
4	10	M	Physical	Step-father	Mexican-American	School Counselor	Injury Report
5	3	M	Physical	Mother	Iranian	School Director	Injury Report
6	7	F	Sexual	Common Law husband	Mexican-American	Mother	Removal of child
7	7	F	Physical	Mother	Mexican-American	School Physician	Removal of child and siblings
8	11	M	Physical	Mother	Black	Aunt and School	Referral to DPSS*
9	14	F	Physical	Father	Mexican-American	School Nurse	Injury Report
10	3,6,8	F,F,M	Physical	Mother	Mexican-American	Grandmother	Active DPSS* Case - Mother was Psychotic

*Department of Public Social Services

35

the next call requiring an officer response to the home or to the school. The first ten cases were included in the sample, and the assumption made that it was a random, non-selected sample.

The general characteristics of the sample were reflective of the random, non-selected sample including the geographic areas, disposition of the complaints, ages of the children, reporting party, type of complaints, characteristics of the parents, and reasons for abuse.

Seven of the eighteen geographic areas in the Los Angeles Police Department were represented in the sample.

Disposition of Cases

The disposition of the investigations were varied. Two case investigations were dismissed by the officers, and no crime report or injury report was made. One case investigation resulted because a neighbor called the police to report a possible child abuse complaint on behalf of a five year old girl. The girl was outside on the front lawn at 10:00 p.m. without supervision and was crying. The police officers investigated the complaint by talking to the neighbor, the mother, and examining the child. There was no evidence of child abuse past or present. Therefore, no injury report nor crime report was filed and no follow-up investigation was planned. When asked how they had reached their decision, they replied, "We make these decisions every day, and it was our judgment that the complaint be dismissed because we did not see any evidence that the child was hurt or was endangered." A second case was also dismissed and a referral made to the Department of Public Social Services for follow-up because the mother was an alcoholic causing neglect and not direct physical abuse. Four injury reports were filed by the officers investigating the complaints. All injury reports require follow-up action by the Abused and Battered Child Unit investigators. In three cases the abused child and siblings were removed from the home. These are reported in Table 6.

family, 1 Iranian family (2 calls on the same child), and 2 black families.

Although little information is known about reporting parties in child abuse cases, it was assumed that the school would report the majority of the cases. When the child goes to school, the exposure to members of the community occurs. Prior to this time, the child has not been subjected to public scrutiny and abuse may remain unreported. Seven of the ten cases were reported by the school, two were reported by family members, one was reported by a neighbor, and none was reported by the Department of Public Social Services irrespective of the mandate by Penal Code 1116.5.

It was important to note that there are nine complaints of physical abuse and one complaint of sexual abuse reported. In five instances of physical abuse the biological mother inflicted the abuse, in two instances the biological father was responsible for the physical abuse, and in two cases a stepfather was responsible. There was no instance where a stepmother or girlfriend inflicted the injury. In the sexual abuse complaint, a 7 year old girl was abused by a common-law husband of the biological mother. He was not related to the girl.

One mother who was abusing her children was overtly psychotic and was also abusing her husband. One mother was an alcoholic, one mother was a gang member who was using drugs regularly, and one mother was pregnant with the possibility of imminent delivery. In one case the mother was colluding with the father who was the abuser even though she did not participate in the abuse. One father said he was disciplining his child because she was participating in gang activities. One father was disturbed because his son was doing poorly in school, wet his bed, and he felt that the grandmother spoiled the child. The child stayed with the grandmother after school while the parents were at work. One father stated that he didn't mean to hurt his child, but had just lost his temper.

Characteristics of Child Abusers and
Those Reporting Child Abuse

Since school personnel are mandated by law to report to the police department suspected child abuse cases, it was not surprising that so many of the cases in this research study were reported by the schools; nonetheless it is interesting that this same law is applicable to the Department of Public Social Services and none of the cases in this study was reported by the Department of Public Social Services.

There were three cases reported by family members. One of the three cases was sexual abuse reported by the mother; one was physical abuse of the children and husband reported by the grandmother. One case was physical abuse and neglect reported by an aunt to the school who then notified the police department. In one case a neighbor reported a suspected case of abuse and neglect which was unfounded. Although the Abused and Battered Child Unit accepts anonymous phone calls reporting abuse, there was none in this study.

School personnel reporting child abuse had an interesting distribution. There were two cases reported by the teachers through the school principal, one by the school principal, one by a school counselor, one by a school nurse, and one by a school physician. Of the ten cases reported, nine were physical abuse complaints and one was sexual abuse.

Parent Variables

Variables regarding parents' background as abused children were identified and are reported in Table 7. In one instance the abusing parent was abused as a child, and in six instances they were not. There were three unknown cases. One abusing parent was not in the home while the police investigation was conducted. Although he was later arrested, information about his background was unavailable to the researcher; another abusing parent was

Table 7

Frequency of Abuse As a Child in the Parent Background**

	Abusing Parent Abused As a Child	Non-Abusing Parent Abused As a Child
Yes	1	0
No	6	6
Unknown	3	4***

N = 13
**May have one or more parents
***Single parent family

overtly psychotic and information about her childhood could not be obtained. The third case was dismissed for lack of evidence and the researcher was unable to obtain information about the background of the suspect. It is important to note that the four cases where the non-abusing parent's background was unknown resulted because the non-abusing parent did not reside in the household (see Table 7).

There was one non-abusing parent who acted as a colluding parent, three single parent families where the father had no contact with the children or the mother, and six non-abusing parents who were not overtly colluding (see Table 8).

The biological mother was found to be the abuser in six of the ten cases involved in this study. The biological father was found to be the abuser in two cases, the stepfather was the abuser in one case, and a common-law husband was the abuser in one instance. This information is presented in Table 9.

Patterns of Abuse

The abuse pattern of the family included in this study indicated that abuse had occurred previously[1] in five of the ten cases,

Table 8

Comparison of Parents Who Were Abused Children to Non-Abused
Children Acting As a Colluding Parent

	Abusing Parent Abused As a Child	Non-Abusing Parent As An Overt Colluding Parent
Yes	1	1
No	6	6
Unknown	3	3

N = 14
**May have one or more parents

Table 9

Family Relationship of Abuser
To Abused Child

	Number of Cases
Biological mother	6
Biological father	2
Stepfather	2
Common-law husband	1

but only one case had been previously reported to the police.[2] Table 10 summarizes the information. In each of the ten cases included in this study, a single instance of child abuse was reported. Yet, when the officers investigated the complaints, they found that in three of the cases multiple abuse had occurred within the family. These patterns are reported in Table 11.

41

Table 10

Police Reporting Pattern of Previous Child Abuse Case

Current Case Police Report of Abuse	Evidence of Previous Abuse (Number of Cases)	
	Yes	No
Previous report	1	0
No previous report	3	5
No police report filed in current investigation	0	1

N = 10

Table 11

Comparison of Single As Opposed to Multiple Siblings Being Abused

Identified Child	Identified 3 Children and Father	Identified Child and Siblings
7	1	2

N = 10

Characteristics of the Police Officer
Investigating Child Abuse Cases

The sample included 19 male officers between the ages of 25 and 39 years of age with an average age of 33. The standard deviation was 3.517. A summary of the demographic data is reported in Table 12. There were 12 white officers, 3 black officers and 4 Hispanic officers, which was similar to the racial mix of police officers employed by the Los Angeles Police Department (see Table 13).

Twelve of the nineteen officers were married and three

Table 12

Demographic Data of 19 Police Officers
Investigating Child Abuse Complaints

Age	
Mean	33
S.D.	3.517
Range	25-39
Ethnic Group	
White	12
Black	3
Hispanic	4
Marital Status	
Single	3
Married	12
Divorced and not remarried	2
Number of Children	
Male	15
Female	9
Total	24
Years with LAPD	
5 or less	10
5 to 10	6
More than 10	3
Rank	
Probationer	2
P-1	0
P-2	14
P-3	3
Education	
High school of equivalent	16
Bachelors degree	3

N = 19

Table 13

A Comparison of the L.A. Police Department Child Abuse Investigators
Included in the Ten Case STudies, by Sex and Ethnic Group

| | Percentage | | Percentage | | | | |
	Male	Female	White	Black	Hispanic	Asian American	American Indian
Departmental	79	2	79	6	10	1	.2
Case Studies	100	0	63	16	21	0	0

N = 19

were single, never having been married. Four of the officers were divorced. Five of the officers who were married or who had been married did not have any children. There were 15 male children and 9 female children, with the youngest child 2 months old, and the oldest child 10 years of age. Six of the officers had two children, one had four children, two officers had three children, and two officers had one child.

The police officers' rank varied from probationer with four months experience to a juvenile officer with twelve years on the job. The officers' average length of time with the police department was six years. Ten of the officers had five or less years with the department; six officers had five to ten years, and five of the officers had ten or more years with the department. There were 14 patrol officers with a P-2 rank, two probationers, two training officers at the P-3 rank.

The educational level of the police officers varied from a high school diploma or equivalent to a bachelor's degree. Sixteen officers had a high school diploma or equivalent, and three officers had bachelor's degrees. Thirteen of the officers had not attended any special schools; six had attended juvenile school; and one had attended special classes at the University of Southern California on child abuse. This information is presented in Table 12.

Decision Making in Child Abuse Investigations

A major role of police officers investigating child abuse complaints is the decision to remove the child from the home in order to protect the child. In this study police officers made decisions to remove the child, to remove the siblings, to arrest one or more of the parents, to admonish parents, to admonish the child, to hospitalize the abusing parent, to dismiss the complaint, and to file an injury report. A summary is presented in Table 14. The observer asked officers how they made their decision, and what criteria they used in reaching those decisions. Out of the ten cases included in this research, nine were based on personal judgment and one was based on the criminal justice code.

In an effort to identify personal judgment criteria, the observer solicited information from the officers investigating the child abuse complaints and found that personal judgments were based on several criteria. In the ten cases included in this study, one decision was based on the appearance of the home, another one on the socioeconomic status of the family, a third was based on an expert opinion, and the fourth decision was based on the officer's conception of the child's need for discipline.

Two cases revealed no evidence of previous abuse, two cases provided evidence of previous abuse, and in another case it was the officer's opinion[3] as to what constituted child abuse. Although the researcher (an expert) was present at all the investigations, there was only one case where an opinion was solicited by the officers doing the investigation.

The researcher rated the decision making approach as rigid or flexible utilizing a Likert scale of 1 to 100 with 1 being rigid and 100 being flexible. The objective-subjective criteria were rated in the same manner with 1 subjective and 100 being objective. The ratings were based on the researcher's observation of the officer's ability to listen and change when objectively appropriate, evidence of anxiety in the officer, and the officer's ability to tolerate ambiguity and disorder in the situation. "Objective" was judged as being capable of an unbiased decision based on the complaint. The mean for rigid-flexible was 34.68 and the mean

45

Table 14

Police Decision Making Process in
Child Abuse Investigations

Type of Decision*		
Removal of child		3
Removal of siblings		2
Arrest parent(s)		2
Admonish parent(s)		2
Admonish child		1
Removal of parent (through hospitalization)		1
Injury report		3
Dismissal of case		3
Criteria for Decision Making		
Criminal justice code		1
Personal judgment		9
Cultural context	0	
Home appearance	1	
S.E.S.	1	
Expert's opinion	1	
Child's need for discipline	1	
Evidence of past abuse	2	
Officer opinion	1	
Role Taken by Officer		
Adversary		3
Facilitator		6
Investigator		8
Observer		2
Type of Interaction		
Supportive		4
Threatening		4
Information giving		1
Investigative		8
Other		2

N = 19

*Officers may make more than one decision in each investigation.

46

for objective-subjective was 56.89 (see Table 15).

Table 15

Police Officers' Approach to Decision Making
in the Ten Case Studies Involving Child
Abuse Complaint Investigations

	Mean
Rigid-Flexible	34.68
Affect	4.68
Objective-Subjective	56.89

N = 19

Role Taken by the Officer in Decision Making

In three instances the officer was perceived by the researcher to assume the role of *adversary*, in six instances the officer was rated as having taken the role of *facilitator*, in eight instances the officer was perceived to have used the role of *investigator* predominantly. In addition, the two probationary officers assumed the role of *observer*. The types of interactions were rated as supportive four times, information giving once, threatening four times, investigative eight times, and in two instances there was silence which was neutral in quality. This information is summarized in Table 14.

The mean score of the interactions on affect was 4.68 on a scale of 0 to 10. The results indicated that 10 of 19 officers responded at the 6, 7, and 8 level of the scale, 9 officers were rated at the 0, 1, 2, 3, and 4 level of the scale. It is important to note that three officers were rated unsatisfactory in their interactions while none was rated as excellent. Six were rated good, six were satisfactory and four were rated poor in their interactions. The results are reported in Table 15.

In seven of the ten cases, the Abused and Battered Child Unit detectives were consulted about the decision to remove the child or to take an injury report. In three instances no consultation was sought by the officer in the field. Officers in one case where the Abused and Battered Child Unit was notified disagreed as to the necessity of notifying the unit. One of the officers stated, "This is clearly not a case of child abuse. Children of this age fall all of the time. I have been an investigator for a long time and have investigated many child abuse cases, and this does not fit the pattern." It was apparent that these two officers did not normally work together and were viewing the situation differently. The second officer disagreed with the first officer and insisted on notifying the unit. This was subsequently a repeat call on the same child. On the first call the child had an injury on the head and stated, "mommy spanked me." On the second call, the next day, the child had a large bandage on his left hand, and when questioned stated, "Daddy took me to the hospital this morning." The nursery school director indicated that the parents claimed that the child had fallen the first day and injured his head, and that the second injury had occurred at the nursery school. The nursery school director and the child's teacher stated that no injury had occurred at school, and they were both concerned for the child's well-being as the parents were visibly upset that the police had been notified of the child's injuries.

Time Factors in Child Abuse Investigations

Time factors reported include the police response time; i.e., how soon after the call did the police respond, the amount of time spent on each response call, and the time lapse between the abuse and the notification of the police. The mean for police response time was 26 minutes with a standard deviation of 14.14. The mean for police investigation time for the initial response was 349 minutes (5.8 hours) with a standard deviation of 204.33. This is reported in Table 16.

Table 16

Time Spent in Child Abuse Complaint
Investigations by Police

	X̄	S.D.
Response Time	26 minutes	14.14
Initial Investigation Time	349 minutes	204.33

N = 10

The time lapse between the occurrence of abuse and notification of the police was reported in increments; less than 30 minutes, 30 to 60 minutes, 1 to 4 hours, 4 hours to 24 hours, and more than 24 hours (see Table 17).

Table 17

Time Lapse Between Abuse and
Notification of Police

Time Lapse	Number
Less than 30 minutes	2
30 minutes to 60 minutes	3
60 minutes to 4 hours	0
4 hours to 24 hours	1
More than 24 hours*	4

N = 10
*Cases picked up by school

Although accurate figures were unavailable indicating when the abuse occurred, estimates were made and reported in Table 16 by the researcher on the basis of information given by the child, the parent, and/or the reporting party.

In one case where the mother was psychotic, the abuse was erratic and occurred at various times. Three cases occurred in the late afternoon after school, two occurred in the late evening, one in the early evening, one in the early morning, and in two cases there was inadequate information to estimate the time of abuse (see Table 18).

Table 18
Approximate Time of Day Abuse Occurred

Time of Day	Number
6 - 9 a.m.	1
9 - 12 a.m.	--
12 - 3 p.m.	--
3 - 6 p.m.	3
6 - 9 p.m.	--
9 - 12 p.m.	3
Eratic*	1
Unknown**	2

N = 10
*Psychotic mother
**Information unavailable

Six Week Follow-Up

At the end of six weeks, the researcher interviewed the investigating officers, examined the police records, and/or made a call to the home in order to determine whether further abuse had occurred as indicated by additional police reports, what method of support had been instituted, what follow-up had been done, and who was doing the follow-up. In addition, it was determined what effect on the family unit the police intervention had; i.e., whether the family remained intact, whether the abused child and siblings were still in the home, and whether the abusing parent remained in the home.

In one case additional abuse[4] occurred as indicated by a second police report; in nine cases no additional police report had been filed. In six cases, the Department of Public Social Services and/or the courts were following the case. In 9 of the 10 cases the abuser remained in the home, and in 6 of the cases, the abused child and the siblings remained in the home. In three cases the police continued to be involved through the courts. This is reported in Table 19.

The results are discussed in Chapter VI. The results of the questionnaire administered to 225 police officers in the Los Angeles Police Department are presented in Chapter V.

CHAPTER FOOTNOTES

[1]Previous abuse was defined as any evidence of previous abuse such as old scars, previous police reports, child or parent stating that abuse had occurred in the past, or any evidence from reporting party.

[2]This case had been reported to the Los Angeles Police Department Abused and Battered Child Unit the previous day.

[3]The officer stated, "This is clearly not a case of child abuse. I have been Investigating these for many years, and know a case of child abuse when I see it."

[4]In order to establish objective criteria to measure additional abuse, the researcher defined additional abuse as an additional police report having been filed. This does not preclude additional abuse but does provide an objective measure.

Table 19

Six Week Follow-Up Summary of the Ten Child Abuse Police Investigations Based on Data Collected Through Review of the Records, Interviews with Officers Attached to the Abused and Battered Child Unit of the L.A.P.D. or Personal Contact with Families

Case	Further Abuse*	Method of Support	Follow-up Being Done	By Whom	Remain in the Home		
					Abusing Parent	Abused Child	Siblings
1	No	None	No		Yes	Yes	Yes
2,5	Yes	Social Worker	Yes	DPSS**	Yes	Yes	Yes
3	No	Social Worker	Yes	DPSS** & Courts	Yes	No	No
4	No	None	No		Yes	Yes	Yes
6	No	Social Worker	Yes	DPSS** & Courts	No	No	None
7	No	Social Worker & Courts	Yes	DPSS** & Courts	Yes	No	No
8	No	Social Worker	Yes	DPSS**	Yes	Yes	None
9	No	None	No		Yes	Yes	Yes
10	No	Social	Yes	DPSS**	Yes	Yes	Yes

*Defined as an additional police report on child abuse.
**Department of Public Social Services

52

CHAPTER V

RESULTS OF THE ATTITUDE QUESTIONNAIRE

In this chapter the results obtained from the questionnaire administered to 225 police officers in the Los Angeles Police Department in conjunction with the ten case studies, reported in Chapter IV are presented. The results of the ten case studies and the 225 police officer's response to the questionnaire are discussed in Chapter VI.

Demographic Data

Those taking part in the study included 225 police officers from the Los Angeles Police Department. There were 117 police officer recruits attending classes at the academy, and 108 experienced police officers who volunteered to complete the questionnaire.

There were 206 male officers and 18 female officers. The age distribution of the participants was as follows: 33 were less than 22 years of age, 141 were 22 to 34 years of age, 48 were 35 to 39 years of age, and 2 were 50 years of age and over. There were 101 with less than 2 years experience, 27 with 2 to 4 years of experience, 43 had 5 to 9 years of experience, and 53 had 10 or more years of experience. This information is summarized in Table 20.

Table 20

Demographic Data on Police Officers
Responding to the Questionnaire

Sex	
Male	206
Female	18
Age*	
Less than 22 years	33
22 to 34 years	141
35 to 50 years	48
More than 50 years	2
Experience As a Police Officer*	
Less than 2 years	101
2 to 4 years	27
5 to 9 years	43
10 or more years	53

N = 224
*Data coded to condense single categories and perserve individual anonymity.

Child Abuse Information Scale

The development of a scale to measure police officers' information level regarding child abuse was one task of this study. Recruit officers' scores positively correlated with the total score on the Child Abuse Information Scale and subscales: Information Regarding Abusing Parents, Abused Child, Role of the Police Officer, Personal History of the Police Officer and General Information About Child Abuse at the .01 level of confidence. This data is summarized and reported in Table 21.

A positive correlation occurred between scores on the Social Responsibility Scale (Berkowitz and Lutterman, 1968), and the Child Abuse Information Scale of experienced police

Table 21

Correlation Coefficients of Recruit Officers, Experienced Officers, Total Officers' Scores on the Child Abuse Information Scale

Variable	Recruit Officers N=117	Experienced Officers N=108	Total Officers N=225
Child Abuse Information Scale			
Abusing Parents Subscale	.389*	.341*	.350*
Abused Child Subscale	.535*	.495*	.515*
Personal History Subscale	.235*	.476*	.369*
Role of Police Officer Subscale	.578*	.614*	.598*
General Information Subscale	.727*	.706*	.717*
Rigidity Scale	.002	-.149**	-.091
Perservative Thinking Subscale	.036	-.009	-.007
Compulsive Doubting Subscale	.164	.050	-.105
Conservatism Subscale	.184**	.084	.074
Anxiety Subscale	-.058	.058	-.054
CSB-1 Scale	.291*	.076	.179**
Short Dogmatism Scale	.014	-.192**	-.077
Social Responsibility Scale	.193**	.154**	.183**
Four Item F-Scale	.011	.044	.023

*Significant at the .01 level of confidence.
**Significant at the .05 level of confidence.

officers which was significant at the .05 level of confidence.

A negative correlation of experienced officers scores obtained on the Rigidity Scale (Rehfisch, 1958) and the Short Dogmatism Scale (Schulze, 1962) proved to be significant at the .05 level of confidence.

The scores of recruit officers and experienced officers on the Short Dogmatism Scale (Schulze, 1962), Social Responsibility Scale (Berkowitz and Lutterman, 1968), and Four Item F Scale (Lane, 1955) when correlated with the Child Abuse Information Scale total scores were not significant (see Table 21). The correlation coefficient of the recruit officer's scores on the CSB-1 Scale (Fass, 1976) and the Child Abuse Information Scale total score was significant at the .01 level of confidence while the correlation coefficient of the experienced officers' was not significant.

An analysis of variance was computed and reported in Table 22 for the individual scales on the Child Abuse Information Scale and the Rigidity Scale (Rehfisch, 1958), Four Item F Scale (Lane, 1955), Social Responsibility Scale (Berkowitz and Lutterman, 1968), and Short Dogmatism Scale (Schulze, 1962). The F-Value obtained was significant at the .01 level of confidence on three of the subscales; Personal History of the Police Officer, Information About the Abused Child, and General Information About Child Abuse. The subscale, The Role of the Police Officer, was found to have an F-Value of 1.978 which is significant at the .05 level of confidence. The subscale, Information About Abusing Parents, was not statistically significant. The Total Child Abuse Information Scale has an F-Value of 2.08 which is significant at the .05 level of confidence.

A correlation coefficient on the Child Abuse Information Scale, CSB-1 Scale (Fass, 1976), Short Dogmatism Scale (Schulze, 1962), Social Responsibility Scale (Berkowitz and Lutterman, 1968), Four Item F Scale (Lane, 1955), and the Rigidity Scale (Rehfisch, 1958) had nine positive correlations and three negative correlations that were significant at the .01 level of confidence (see Table 23). There were six positive correlations at the .05 level of confidence. Positive correlations were scores on the

Table 22

Analysis of Variance - Child Abuse Information Subscales with Rigidity
Scale, Four Item F Scale, Social Responsibility Scale,
CSB-1 Scale and Short Dogmatism Scale

Variable	df	S.S.	M.S.	F-Value	P
Personal History of the	9	87.530	9.726	2.61	.01
Police Officer Subscale	215	800.025	3.721		
Abused Child Information	9	143.501	15.945	2.61	01
Subscale	215	1308.499	6.086		
Abusing Parent Information	9	21.063	2.340	.62	NS
Subscale	215	806.697	3.752		
Role of the Police Officer	9	162.620	18.059	1.98	.05
Information Subscale	215	1964.740	9.138		
General Information about	9	242.340	26.927	2.91	.01
Child Abuse Subscale	215	1992.300	9.266		
Total	9	838.448	93.161	2.08	.05
	215	9611.934	44.707		

N = 225

Table 23

Correlation Coefficient Matrix - Child Abuse Information Scale, CSB-1 Scale, Dogmatism Scale
Social Responsibility Scale, and Authoritarianism Scale

	1	2	3	4	5	6	7	8	9
Total Child Abuse Information Scale									
1. Information about the Abusing Parent	-	.034	.038	-.055	.150**	.015	-.033	.006	-.030
2. Information about the Abused Child			-.014	.128**	.172**	.063	.105	-.019	.298*
3. Personal History of the Police Officer				.037	.141**	-.008	.167**	.180*	-.032
4. Role of Police Officer					.238*	.242	.013	.122	-.031
5. General Information about Child Abuse						.097	.139**	.175*	-.122
6. CSB-1 Scale							.111	.269*	-.121
7. Dogmatism Scale								-.08	.343*
8. Social Responsibility Scale									.050
9. Authoritarianism Scale									--

N = 225
*Significant at the .01 level of confidence.
**Significant at the .05 level of confidence.

58

Information About Abusing Parent and the subscale General Information About Child Abuse. Scores on the Abused Child Information Scale and the Four Item F-Scale were significant at the .01 level of confidence while the scores on Information About Abused Child, Role of the Police Officer, and General Information About Child Abuse was significant at the .05 level of confidence. Scores on the subscale Personal History of the Police Officer, scores on the Social Responsibility Scale (Berkowitz and Lutterman, 1968) and scores on the Rigidity Scale (Rehfisch, 1958) were positively correlated and were significant at the .01 level of confidence. Scores on the Personal History of Police Officer, scores on the General Information About Child Abuse, and Short Dogmatism Scale (Schulze, 1962) scores were positively correlated and were significant at the .05 level of confidence (see Table 23).

The scores on the subscales Role of the Police Officer, General Information About Child Abuse, and the CSB-1 Scale (Fass, 1976) were significant at the .01 level of confidence. While scores on the subscale General Information About Child Abuse positively correlated with scores on the Social Responsibility Scale (Berkowitz and Lutterman, 1968), and the Rigidity Scale (Rehfisch, 1958) at the .01 level of confidence. Scores on the Short Dogmatism Scale (Schulze, 1962) and the General Information About Child Abuse Scale indicated a positive correlation at the .05 level of confidence. The scores on the CSB-1 Scale (Fass, 1976) and Social Responsibility Scale (Berkowitz and Lutterman, 1968) correlated at the .01 level of confidence (see Table 23).

Short Dogmatism Scale (Schulze, 1962) scores and Rigidity Scale (Rehfisch, 1958) scores were highly correlated at the .01 level of confidence. The scores on the Social Responsibility Scale (Berkowitz and Lutterman, 1968) and the Rigidity Scale (Rehfishch, 1958) indicated a negative correlation at the .01 level of confidence while scores on the Four Item F Scale (Lane, 1955) and Rigidity Scale (Rehfisch, 1958) scores indicated a positive correlation that was significant at the .01 level of confidence. These are reported in Table 23.

There were 13 multiple correlations that were significant at the .01 level of confidence when a multiple regression statistical analysis was used to examine the relationship between scores obtained on the Four Item F Scale (Lane, 1955), Rigidity Scale (Rehfisch, 1958), CSB-1 Scale (Fass, 1976), Short Dogmatism Scale (Schulze, 1962), and Social Responsibility Scale (Berkowitz and Lutterman, 1968), and scores obtained on the subscales of the Child Abuse Information Scale; Information About the Abusing Parent, Information About the Abused Child, Personal History of the Police Officer, and General Information About Child Abuse.

The five relationships were: CSB-1 Scale (Fass, 1976) and Information About the Abused Child; Social Responsibility Scale (Berkowitz and Lutterman, 1968) and General Information About Child Abuse; Social Responsibility Scale (Berkowitz and Lutterman, 1968) and Information About the Abused Child (see Table 24).

Four positive correlation coefficients were found to be significant at the .01 level of confidence. Three of the correlations were between the Rigidity Scale (Rehfisch, 1958), the Short Dogmatism Scale (Schulze, 1962), and the Four Item F Scale (Lane, 1955). The fourth positive correlation was between the Short Dogmatism Scale (Schulze, 1962) and the Four Item F Scale (Lane, 1955). In addition, a negative correlation between scores on the Rigidity Scale (Rehfisch, 1958) and the Social Responsibility Scale (Berkowitz and Lutterman, 1968) correlated at the .01 level of confidence. This is reported in Table 25.

A multiple regression statistical technique was used to examine relationships between scores on the Four Item F Scale (Lane, 1955), Rigidity Scale (Rehfisch, 1958), CSB-1 Scale (Fass, 1976), Short Dogmatism Scale (Schulze, 1962), and Social Responsibility Scale (Berkowitz and Lutterman, 1968) in recruit officers at the Los Angeles Police Department Academy and experienced officers in the Los Angeles Police Department. None was found to be statistically significant. The results are reported in Table 26.

In order to identify any differences between experienced

60

Table 24

Multiple Regression Summary -- Child Abuse Information Scale

	Dependent Variables									
	Abusing Parents		Abused Child		Personal History		Role of Police Officer		General Information	
Variable	M.R.	p	M.R.	p	M.R.	p	M.R.	p	M.R.	p
Four Item F Scale	.03	--	.30	.01	.03	--	.03	--	.12	--
Rigidity Scale	.10	--	.30	.01	.16	--	.04	--	.20	--
CSB-1 Scale	.14	--	.31	.01	.24	.05	.26	.01	.29	.01
Short Dogmatism Scale	.15	--	.31	.01	.28	.01	.27	.01	.30	.01
Social Responsibility Scale	.16	--	.31	.01	.31	.01	.28	.01	.32	.01

N = 225

Table 25

Correlation Coefficient Matrix
Rigidity Scale, CSB-1 Scale, Short Dogmatism Scale,
Social Responsibility Scale, and Four Item F Scale

	1**	2	3	4	5
1. Rigidity Scale	--	.002	.391*	-.199*	.260*
2. CSB-1 Scale			.110	.269*	.121
3. Short Dogmatism Scale				-.078	.343*
4. Social Responsibility Scale					-.05
5. Four Item F Scale					--

N = 225
*Significant at the .01 level of confidence.
**Each number horizontally corresponds to the number next to the name of the scale vertically.

Table 26

Multiple Regression Summary of Child Abuse Information Scale
A-Academy Police Officer Recruits, B-Experienced Police Officers,
and C-Total

Variable	Recruits[A]		Experienced Officers[B]		Total[C]	
	M.R.	p	M.R.	p	M.R.	p
Four Item F. Scale	.01	--	.04	--	.023	--
Rigidity Scale	.01	--	.18	--	.102	--
Perservative Thinking	.03	--	.19	--	.107	--
Compulsive Doubting	.16	--	.21	--	.163	--
Conservatism	.24	--	.21	--	.189	--
Anxiety	.24	--	.24	--	.193	--
CSB-1 Scale	.31	--	.24	--	.233	--
Short Dogmatism Scale	.31	--	.30	--	.254	--
Social Responsibility Scale	.34	--	.295	--	.254	--

A - N = 117
B - N = 108
C - N = 225

officers and recruit officers, a t-test of difference between means was done and is reported in Table 27. No differences were found. An analysis of variance was done yielding an F-Value (df 9,107) of 1.554 for Recruits and an F-Value (df 9,98) of 1.163 for Experienced Officers, which were not statistically significant at the .05 level of confidence. The F-Value for the total scores was 2.084, which was significant at the .05 level of confidence with 9,215 degrees of freedom.

Table 27

Analysis of Variance* - Child Abuse Information Scale with Rigidity Scale, Four Item F Scale, Social Responsibility Scale, CSB-1 Scale, and Short Dogmatism Scale with A-Police Officer Recruits, B-Experienced Police Officers and C-Total

	Source	df	SS	MS	F	P
Recruits	Scales	9	554.773	61.641	1.554	N.S.
	Subjects	107	4141.458	39.649		
Experienced Officers	Scales	9	540.864	60.096	1.163	N.S.
	Subjects	98	5062.571	51.658		
Total	Scales	9	838.448	93.161	2.084	.05
	Subjects	215	9611.934	44.707		

N = 225
*Repeated Measures Design

A Comparison of Police Officers Completing the Child Abuse Questionnaire and Police Officers Investigating the Ten Child Abuse Complaints Included in This Study

The average age of police officers included in the sample of officers investigating child abuse was 33, and the average estimated age, categories collapsed to maintain anonymity, was 28 years. The percentage of male officers investigating child abuse cases was 100% while the sample of police officers completing the Child Abuse Questionnaire consisted of 91% male and 9% female.

Data on the average length of time on the police department was collapsed into categories and 52% of the officers involved in child abuse investigations in the field had been with the Los Angeles Police Department less than five years, and of the officers answering the questionnaire, 57% had been with the department for less than five years. Of the officers in the ten case studies, 32% had been with the department for 5 to 9 years while 19% of the officers completing the questionnaires had been with the police department for 5 to 9 years. Of the officers in the ten case studies, 16% had ten or more years with the Los Angeles Police Department, and 24% of the field officers answering the questionnaire had ten or more years with the Los Angeles Police Department. The correlation between police officers in the ten case studies and police officers completing the questionnaire on length of time on the department was .84 which is significant at the .01 level of confidence (see Table 28).

A discussion and integration of the results of the ten case studies and the questionnaire is presented in Chapter VII.

Table 28

Percentage Comparison of Police Officer Sample Investigating Child
Abuse Complaints and Police Officer Sample Completing Child
Abuse Questionnaire

	10 Case Studies %	Child Abuse Questionnaire %
Sex		
Male	100	91
Female	0	9
Length of Time on Los Angeles Police Department*		
Less than 5 years	52	57
5 to 9 years	32	19
10 or more years	16	24

N = 224
*Correlation .84 which is significant at the .01 level of confidence.

CHAPTER VI

DISCUSSION

This study was designed to examine the police officer's role in the initial police response to child abuse complaints. The research design included both a descriptive naturalistic field study and comparative statictical correlations. The study was conducted at the Los Angeles Police Department.

There were 10 case studies in which the researcher accompanied police officers investigating the initial child abuse complaints involving 19 police officers and 12 children.

In addition to these case studies, 225 police officers completed a Child Abuse Questionnaire measuring attitudes of rigidity, authoritarianism, dogmatism, compulsivity, social responsibility, and information about child abuse. The sample included 108 experienced police officers and 117 police officer recruits from the Los Angeles Police Department.

The data were analyzed using means, standard deviations, t-tests, analyses of variance, multiple correlations, and simple correlations.

This discussion consists of three sections: (1) the results of the 10 case studies including the general characteristics of the sample, demographic data, characteristics of the families involved in child abuse complaints, data regarding the reporting party, characteristics of the police officers investigating child abuse complaints, the results of the six week follow-up, and most importantly, *characteristic bases for a judgment of child abuse on the part of the investigating officers;* (2) the results of an attitude survey of 225 police officers completing the child abuse questionnaire; and (3) a comparison of the demographic data obtained in the case studies with the questionnaire data.

Discussion of the Ten Case Studies

Types of Abuse
The majority (90%) of the child abuse cases included in this study involved physical abuse which supports the literature proposing that physical abuse of children is more commonly reported than sexual abuse (Helfer and Kempe, 1974). The ethnic groups were varied and included white, black, Iranian, and Hispanic indicating child abuse occurs in all ethnic groups.

Age and Sex of Abused Child
A general consensus that child abuse occurs in a wide range of ages and in both sexes was supported in this study. The age range of the abused children was 1 year to 15 years old and involved 6 females and 6 males.

Disposition by Police
Howell (1979) indicated police officers normally leave abused and battered children and their siblings in the home under the supervision of the Department of Public Social Services, which proved to be true in this sample since only 30% of the investigations led to the removal of children from their families. Information like this may serve to mitigate the fear that responding officers in uniform disrupt the family unit and interfere with parents' rights (Strauss, Gelles, and Steinmetz, 1976) by removing the

children.

Another parameter this study examined was the disposition of the complaint. As a result of police investigations, four injury reports were filed, three abused children and their siblings were removed from the home, one abusing parent was taken to the hospital since she was overtly psychotic, and in one case no report was filed. This indicates that a variety of dispositions are being made by the police officers in the field based on situational factors and personal judgment.

Reporting of Cases

The schools reported the majority of the cases to the police. This may have occurred in part because the study was limited to abuse cases where patrol officers went to the home or to the school to investigate child abuse complaints.

Family members reported 30% of the child abuse while neighbors reported 10%. This finding indicates family and neighbors were an important source of concern for the abused child.

The Department of Public Social Services is mandated by law to report suspected child abuse cases in California. However, none of the cases included in this study was reported by them. This may have resulted from the fact that in the Los Angeles Police Department officers assigned to the Abused and Battered Child Unit investigate cases where no immediate emergency situations exist, where patrol cars are dispatched for emergency calls. The Department of Public Social Services workers may already have made an intervention as well as a judgment that the child was not in imminent danger. The police Abused and Battered Child Unit was also limited in type and number of cases they investigate due to limited personnel.

Parent Variables in Child Abuse

The literature indicates that abusing parents were often

abused as children. However, the results of this study did not support this hypothesis as only 10% of the abusing parents reported they had been abused as children. This may have been a result of the sampling technique or it may indicate that parents who abuse their children but do not cause injuries requiring hospitalization are different from abusing parents whose children's injuries require hospitalization.

The abuse in 80% of the cases was done by the biological parents with the biological mother being the abuser 60% of the time. From this data *it appears that information regarding child growth and development may be lacking in these parents as well as an inability to tolerate the frustrations created by their children.* One stepfather abused his stepson because the child received poor grades in school; one father wanted to teach his daughter to not participate in gang activities; another father stated he just got so mad at his son when he disobeyed him that "he lost his cool." This tends to support the theory that abusing parents have low frustration levels and act on their impulses without considering the consequences of their actions.

Data collected in this study indicates that abused children are victims of violence on an ongoing basis. In 50% of the cases, the evidence of previous abuse was present, and in one case there had been a prior police report of suspected child abuse. Although one child is often selected in the family to be the victim or scapegoat (Helfer and Kempe, 1974), the data in this study indicated that multiple abuse occurred in 30% of the cases. Again, the sample of parents who do not abuse their children enough to cause hospitalization may be different from that of abusing parents whose abused children require hospitalization. It appears these parents have enough control to stop themselves before doing severe damage to their children.

Intervention with parents at an early stage of the child's development might prevent physical and psychological damage to the child. Many of the parents in this study appear to be lacking in parenting skills as well as easily frustrated by their children. These parents as children have learned to control children through the use of physical force. This may be the beginning of a continuous cycle of child abuse for generations to come unless effective interventions are made.

A program designed to educate parents through television might prove effective in teaching parents what to expect from their children as well as provide parents with information regarding safe, effective methods of discipline.

Characteristics of the Police Officers Conducting Child Abuse Investigations

Police officers are mandated by law to investigate suspected child abuse cases and are often the first person with authority to interact with the family involved in child abuse. Therefore, the major focus of this study was on the police officer investigating child abuse complaints.

Decision making is a major role of the police officer, and data obtained on the decision making process in cases observed for this study was categorized as (1) type of decision made, (2) criteria for decision making, (3) role taken by officer, and (4) the type of interaction. *In this study 90% of the decisions were based on the personal judgment of the police officer while 10% were based on the criminal justice code.*

On the basis of this information it becomes imperative that police officers investigating child abuse complaints have an understanding of parenting skills, growth and development patterns, and issues involving family dynamics as their information could then be utilized in the crisis situation. In addition to this knowledge, police officers need to have skills in communication and crisis intervention techniques.

In 4 of the 19 interactions studied, police officers were defined as being threatening (threatening interactions were either to admonish the parent, child, or to locate a sibling of an abused child in order to take the sibling into protective custody). At one point during the last interaction the police officer stated, "We should never have become this involved; we should have let the

70

Abused and Battered Child Unit handle this part." This may indicate that the officer did not like the threatening role he had assumed, that he disliked child abuse investigations or that he disliked the amount of work he had to put in on the case. The investigation of this case took 16 hours from the initial call to the disposition of the case.

Since the role of the police officer includes investigation of child abuse complaints, it was not surprising to learn that 47% of the time the officers included in this study assumed the *role of investigator*. They assumed the *role of facilitator* 32% of the time, *adversary role* 16% of the time, and as an *observer role* 10% of the time. It appears that in the majority of situations involving child abuse investigations, police officers are fulfilling the role prescribed to them by society. Two probationary level officers with four months experience assumed the role of observer. This would be expected because they were learning their role through observation of the performance of a training officer.

The adversary role resulted when officers were trying to locate a sibling of an abused child. The two officers investigating the case assumed two disparate roles, one was that of the adversary and the other was that of the facilitator. The explanation for their procedure was, "We need to use whatever means we can in order to locate the child." The sibling was with the father who was the abuser; the mother was afraid her husband would be arrested and her child taken away. Consequently, in this case, she was willing to go to jail in order to protect the father.

In a second case where both officers assumed the role of adversary, the child had been participating in gang activities. The officers stated to the girl, "Your father went too far with the discipline, but you are not to use this as a threat to your father when he tries to discipline you. We don't want to have you running to the police using this as a reason for not obeying your father. He has your best interest at heart. You know what can happen to you in those gangs." With this kind of input, it would seem that the child would be very reluctant to report any additional abuse as the officers had almost sanctioned the discipline she had received. It appears the officer's knowledge of gang

71

activities and the outcome of being a part of a gang influenced their judgment in this situation. Their lack of knowledge that abused children are prone to take responsibility for the abuse they receive may have been detrimental to their decision making process.

Generally, the *officer's approach to decision making* indicated a *tendency toward rigidity* as evidenced by a mean score in the upper quatrile. The mean score on the objective-subjective criteria indicated a *balance between the use of objective and subjective criteria in decision making.*

Interactions were rated on a 1 to 10 scale in regard to Affect, and the mean was 4.68. Although the Affect was in the middle range of the scale, there was a skewed distribution of the ratings since 21% of the officers were rated as being poor in their interactions while none of the officers was rated as being superior. Scores were obviously skewed toward the "poor interactions." It would appear from the data in this sample that *training to enhance police officer's communication with abused children, their families, and those individuals reporting child abuse would improve the officer's interactions* with families involved in child abuse.

Summary of the Ten Case Studies

In the ten case studies included in this study, physical abuse occurred more often than sexual abuse. Abuse occurred in both sexes across a wide spectrum of ages, different ethnic backgrounds, and abused children were victims of violence on an ongoing basis. Much of the abuse may have resulted because the abusing parents had low frustration levels and were lacking in information regarding child growth and development.

Time Considerations in Child Abuse Investigations

The police initial response time to a child abuse complaint call averaged 26 minutes which indicates that *child abuse investigations were viewed as being important to the Los Angeles Police Department.*

Data collected regarding the approximate time of day child abuse occurred revealed that 60% occurred between 3:00 p.m. and 9:00 p.m. This is the time of day when mothers who were responsible for 60% of the child abuse in this study may be busy with household chores such as preparing dinner, cleaning up, and the time of day when their frustration level may have been low. It is also the time of day when many mothers, fathers, and boyfriends return home from work. *The children may then become the objects of displaced frustrations encountered during the day.*

In this study officers frequently stated that children who are taken into custody are often back in the home before they have completed the paperwork on the case. Officers in this study averaged 5.8 hours on each child abuse complaint investigation with the range of 30 minutes to 16 hours. This data suggests that *police officer morale may be affected by the inordinate amount of time police officers spend on child abuse investigations without any subsequent feedback on the case.*

Six Week Follow-Up on the Ten Cases in this Study

The follow-up data indicated that additional abuse had occurred in one instance involving a second police report, but that in 90% of the cases no evidence or police report of additional child abuse existed. This may be because once the police have intervened the parents no longer abuse their children, or it may be after the initial interaction with the police the family was better able to hide the abuse. The family may have reconstituted itself into a protective circle preventing interference by outsiders.

In 60% of the cases the abused child and the siblings remained in the home. In 70% of the cases, the police assigned to the Abused and Battered Child Unit of the Los Angeles Police Department, the Department of Public Social Services, and/or the courts continued to be involved with the families. *Of the cases, 30% were not being followed by any public or private agency.* Although it appears that follow-up was adequate in the majority of the cases in this study, the question of continued abuse of the children who were not being followed by any public agency is an issue professionals need to address.

Child Abuse Questionnaire Responses

Another dimension of this study involved the administration of a Child Abuse Questionnaire developed by the researcher to police officers in the Los Angeles Police Department. The sample included both experienced officers and inexperienced officers. The majority of the officers were male (91%) with the majority under 34 years of age. More than half (57%) of the officers had less than 5 years experience as a police officer. This sample, therefore, conforms to Collie's (1975) contention *that young relatively inexperienced police officers are handling the majority of the child abuse investigations.*

Discussion of the Results of the Questionnaire Administered to 225 Police Officers in the Los Angeles Police Department

A child abuse questionnaire was developed in order to study the relationship between the officer's level of child abuse information, rigidity, authoritarianism, compulsivity, social responsibility and dogmatism. The correlation coefficient of the Rigidity Scale (Rehfisch, 1958) scores and the Child Abuse Information subscale Personal History of the Police Officer had a negative correla-

74

tion of -.156 which is significant at the .05 level of confidence. Correlation coefficients between rigidity scores and general information about child abuse subscale scores had a negative correlation of -.189 which is significant at the .01 level of confidence. These results may indicate rigid police officers may also have inadequate information regarding child abuse issues. Nonetheless, it should be noted that these correlations while significant only accounted for 1½% to 3½% of the variance.

It was interesting to note that a negative correlation existed between experienced officers' total scores on the Child Abuse Information scale, and the scores on the Rigidity Scale (Rehfisch, 1958) and did not exist in the scores of inexperienced officer recruits at the Los Angeles Police Department Academy (see Table 21). In addition the total score for both experienced and inexperienced officers was not statistically significant. This may indicate that police officers tend to become more rigid as they gain more experience as a police officer. It may also indicate that people who have recently chosen to be police officers and were attending the police academy at the time this study was completed are less rigid in their attitudes and have more information about child abuse issues than police officers who are presently patrol officers in the Los Angeles Police Department and participated in the study. Police officers may become cynical after being exposed to the criminal segment of the population over a period of time and this may account for the difference in attitudes.

Another area studied involves examining the level of information on child abuse issues and police officers' sense of social responsibility. It was predicted that a positive correlation would occur between scores on the Social Responsibility Scale (Berkowitz and Lutterman, 1968) and scores on the Child Abuse Information Scale. It was interesting that recruit officers' scores on the Social Responsibility Scale (Berkowitz and Lutterman, 1968) and the Child Abuse Information Scale correlated at the .05 level of confidence while experienced officers' scores on these same scales were not statistically significant. This may indicate that recruit officers have more information about child abuse issues and/or are more socially sensitive than experienced officers in the field.

A third area involved examining the relationship of police officers' attitudes toward rigidity, social responsibility, compulsivity, dogmatism, and authoritarianism through correlating scores on the Rigidity Scale (Rehfisch, 1958), Short Dogmatism Scale (Schulze, 1962), CSB-1 Scale (Fass, 1976), and the Social Responsibility Scale (Berkowitz and Lutterman, 1968). Positive correlations between scores on all of these scales were expected, however, they did not occur. There was a significant correlation of scores on five of the measures; a negative correlation was found between scores on the Social Responsibility Scale (Berkowitz and Lutterman, 1968) and Rigidity Scale (Rehfisch, 1958) which was significant at the .01 level of confidence. There were four positively correlated measures significant at the .01 level of confidence: scores on the Rigidity Scale (Rehfisch, 1958) and the Short Dogmatism Scale (Schulze, 1962); and the Four Item F-Scale (Lane, 1955); and scores on the CSB-1 Scale (Fass, 1976), and the Social Responsibility Scale (Berkowitz and Lutterman, 1968). No other correlations were significant. None of the multiple regression correlations were statistically significant; therefore, the hypothesis that for this police group rigidity, authoritarianism, dogmatism, compulsivity, and social responsibility have a significant positive correlation was rejected.

The lack of a significant positive correlation between scores on the CSB-1 Scale (Fass, 1976) and the Rigidity Scale (Rehfisch, 1958) scores suggest the two scales measure different areas of compulsivity. Fass (1976) found in her study of college students at Cal Tech that the CSB-1 Scale failed to differentiate high level compulsives from low level compulsives and attributed it to the sample she used. It may be possible that police officers in this sample were not representative of the police officer population.

From the data collected in this study, it would appear that highly compulsive police officers have a greater sense of social responsibility than rigid impulsive police officers. It also appears that highly rigid police officers are more dogmatic, authoritarian, and impulsive than less rigid police officers.

Child abuse investigations are tedious and time consuming.

They require meticulous attention to detail, an ability to persevere, plus empathy and concern for both the parents and the children involved.

The dogmatic, authoritarian, rigid police officer may have a difficult time relating to families involved in child abuse investigations because the officer would probably find it hard to understand the parents' inability to control their actions. They may also be intolerant of other people's opinions. This might be detrimental to abused children and their families and could result in the families deferring help from outside sources because of the feelings of inadequacy generated by officers. Therefore, the highly compulsive police officer with a sense of social responsiblity may be the most effective police officer in child abuse investigations.

Comparison of the Two Samples of the Police Officers' Demographic Data

The literature indicates that young inexperienced police officers investigate the majority of child abuse complaints. This was true in this study; the average age of the police officer investigating the child abuse complaint was 33 years and the range was 25 to 39. Ten of the officers had less than 5 years experience, and the average was 6 years with a range from 4 months to 12 years. Two police officers with four months experience were riding with training officers in order to learn police procedures. Collie (1974) indicates that young officers are assigned to more experienced officers in order to learn police procedure in child abuse investigations, and Preiss and Ehrlich (1966) propose that young officers chose a more experienced officer as a role model. The data in this study supports both of these contentions.

Although 2% of the police officers in the Los Angeles Police Department are female, and 9% of the officers responding to questions on the questionnaire were female, only 25% of the female officers are field qualified. The majority are investigators in special assignments. The 9% included in the sample are not all assigned to patrol duty. The Los Angeles Police Department has been mandated by the courts to increase the number of female officers. The percentage of women included in the sample is higher than the percentage of women officers employed by the Los Angeles Police Department which was a reflection of this effort rather than a selected sample. Female recruit officers included in this sample will probably be assigned to patrol cars when they complete their training.

If they are knowledgeable in child abuse issues and properly trained in investigative methods, they may have a special opportunity to protect children from abuse by their parents since the presence of a female may make the parents less defensive and the child more open as the public views women as more nurturing and less aggressive than males. This could benefit both the abused child and their parents. Since the family is more open to change in a crisis situation and the female officer is less threatening, suggestions for counseling and parent training may be more acceptable to the family.

Although this study did not examine differences between male and female police officer's attitudes toward rigidity, dogmatism, compulsivity, authoritarianism, and levels of child abuse information, the information might be useful in designing a training program. The training could benefit both the male and female officer by teaching the officers to utilize their own unique attributes, and to recognize their partner's attributes.

In summary, it appears that the sample of officers involved in the child abuse investigation case studies and officers included in the sample answering questions on the questionnaire are closely related as data obtained correlated (.84) at the .001 level of confidence.

Implications for Future Research

The major focus of this study was on the initial police call in child abuse investigations and was, therefore, limited in scope. However, the results of this study raised several questions regarding child abuse.

There appeared to be a difference between the results of this study and the literature in relation to the characteristics of abusing parents. This may be a result of the small sample. It would be helpful to know if there is a difference between abusing parents whose abused children require hospitalization and abusing parents who do not abuse their children enough to require hospitalization. This type of information would be a valuable contribution since it could be used to institute training programs designed to impact parents of both groups. It may be that parents whose discipline does not inflict child injuries requiring hospitalization do not view themselves as child abusers and do not seek help or counseling when appeals are made to child abusers through the media.

In this study referrals were made by officers to the Department of Public Social Services and a check revealed that follow-up was being done by that agency. It is important to know what impact a referral to the Department of Public Social Services has on the family. Does abuse continue to occur? Does the family remain intact?

What are the effects on the child who is removed from the family? Does the length of time away from the family influence the child's development?

Family members and neighbors were an important resource to the abused children in this study. What prompted family members or neighbors to call the police on behalf of the child, and what role do they play in the family constellation?

When child abuse occurs and is reported to the police, the officer intervenes and investigates the complaint. Little is known regarding the role of the police officer in the initial child abuse complaint. This study has made a contribution to that body of knowledge, and has raised additional questions that need to be answered. One such question involves the value of training police officers in child abuse issues. Are there differences in police officers' approaches to child abuse investigations after receiving training in child abuse issues such as growth and development, family dynamics, cultural practices in child rearing, parenting skills, communication, and crisis intervention techniques?

Women are becoming police officers at an ever increasing rate. There is a question about possible differences in approach of male and female officers investigating child abuse complaints. Are there differences between male and female officers in attitudes involving rigidity, authoritarianism, dogmatism, social responsibility, compulsivity and child abuse information levels.

Because of the small sample size, it is important to replicate this study in order to validate the findings and perhaps identify a child abuse information cluster that would facilitate selection and training of police officers to investigate child abuse complaints.

It would be valuable to do a longitudinal study where interviews with the children in this sample were conducted in one year, two years, five years, and ten years in order to determine what effect the police intervention had on their lives.

This study did not focus on the family; however, an additional study that would be valuable would include an in depth interview of family members either the same day or within a week of the initial intervention by the police in order to study the dynamics of child abusing families while they are still receptive to outside help with an exploratory approach.

An evaluation research study involving the implementation of some immediate interventions for the family by a social agency to determine whether treatment within the six to eight week period would be effective in preventing additional child abuse.

Decision making is a major role of the police officer; it would be valuable to know what effect a partner has on the decision making process. What process do partners utilize in formulating a decision to either remove the child or to leave the child in the home.

Another study might entail a comparison of officers who have had special training in child abuse investigations and work in the specialized unit of the Abused and Battered Child Unit of the Los Angeles Police Department and officers who are on patrol duty without special training. It would be helpful to know if any differences exist and how these are reflected in the decision making process. For example, do personality differences exist between officers in the specialized unit and officers in other units, and do changes in attitudes of police officers occur over a period of time? Do changes in attitudes of police officers who spend two months on special assignment to the Abused and Battered Child Unit occur? What effect does continuous exposure to the investigations of child abuse have on officers who spend years on the unit; i.e., does burn-out occur?

Professionals in the field are seeking answers that will prevent the occurrences of child abuse. Children are our future, and they deserve our protection. Hopefully, this study has made a small addition to the growing body of knowledge regarding child abuse.

CHAPTER VII

SUMMARY AND CONCLUSIONS

The purpose of this study was twofold: (1) to describe what happens during the initial investigation of child abuse complaints through the analyses of ten case studies, and (2) the administration of a questionnaire to 225 police officers (108 experienced officers and 117 recruit officers) of the Los Angeles Police Department. The questionnaire was designed to measure attitudes toward rigidity, social responsibility, dogmatism, authoritarianism, compulsivity and levels of information regarding child abuse. A comparison was then made between experienced officers and recruit officers.

A systems model of role theory developed by Gross, Mason, and MacEachern (1966) was used to examine the role of the police officer during the initial investigation of a child abuse complaint.

Results of the ten case studies were analyzed using means and standard deviations. Results of the questionnaire were statistically analyzed using analyses of variance, multiple correlation, simple correlations, and t-tests.

Analyses of the ten case studies indicated that physical abuse was more commonly reported to the police than sexual abuse, biological parents from different ethnic backgrounds abused their children on an ongoing basis. This was probably due to the parents' inability to tolerate the frustrations and their lack of parenting skills. The majority of the child abuse occurred between 3:00 p.m. and 9:00 p.m. to children from 1 year old to 15 years old. In a follow-up study six weeks after the initial police intervention, 60% of the abused children remained in the home.

Police officers' initial response time to child abuse calls averaged 26 minutes, and officers averaged 5.8 hours spent on each child abuse complaint.

Positive correlations were expected between scores on the Rigidity Scale (Rehfisch, 1958), Short Dogmatism Scale (Schulze, 1962), CSB-1 Scale (Fass, 1976), Social Responsibility Scale (Berkowitz and Lutterman, 1968), and Four Item F-Scale (Lane, 1955) but did not occur. The hypothesis that a significant positive correlation would occur was rejected. Other relationships were identified in the results including a relationship between rigidity, dogmatism and authoritarianism.

It appears from the data collected in this study, young relatively inexperienced male police officers investigate child abuse complaints in the city of Los Angeles. Child abuse investigations are time consuming and tedious requiring a large investment of the officer's time. In a comparison of experienced and recruit officers, recruit officers scored higher on the Social Responsibility Scale (Berkowitz and Lutterman, 1968) and had a higher score on the Child Abuse Information Scale than experienced officers.

REFERENCES

REFERENCES

Aquilera, D., Messeck, J., and Farrell, M. *Crisis intervention theory and methodology.* St. Louis: The C. V. Mosby Company, 1970.

Auerbach, S., and Kilmann, P. Crisis intervention: a review of outcome research. *Psychological Bulletin,* 1977, 84, 1189-1217.

Bard, M. *The function of police in crisis intervention and conflict management.* Washington, D.C.: Criminal Justice Associates, Inc., 1975. (a)

Bard, M. Collaboration between law enforcement and the social sciences. *Professional Psychology,* May 1975, 127-134. (b)

Bard, M., and Berkowitz, B. A community psychology consultation program in police family crisis intervention. *International Journal of Social Psychiatry,* 1969, 15, 209-215.

Barocas, H. Urban policemen: crisis mediators or crisis creators? *American Journal of Orthopsychiatry,* 1973, 43, 632-639.

Bellak, L. *Handbook of community psychiatry and community mental health.* NY: Grune and Stratton, Inc., 1964.

Berkowitz, L., and Lutterman, K. The traditionally socially responsible personality. *Public Opinion Quarterly*, 1968, 32, 169-185.

Biddle, B., and Thomas, E. *Role theory concepts and research.* NY: John Wiley & Sons, Inc., 1966.

California Penal Code Section 11116.6. Deerings, 1978.

Caplan, G. *Principles of preventive psychiatry.* NY: Basic Books, Inc., 1964.

Child abuse and neglect. The problem and its management. The roles and responsibility of professionals. Washington, D.C.: U.S. Department of Health Education and Welfare, Children's Bureau National Center on Child Abuse and Neglect, 1977.

Collie, J. The police role. In A. W. Franklin (Ed.) *Concerning child abuse.* Edinburg, Scotland: Churchill Livingston, 1975.

Collins, J. The role of the law enforcement agency. In R. Helfer and C. Kempe (Eds.), *The battered child.* Chicago: University of Chicago Press, 1974.

Dean, C. *Summation of critical issues for social scientists working with police agencies.* NY: Human Sciences Press, 1975.

Delinquency rehabilitation report. Washington, D.C.: U.S. Department of Health, Education and Welfare by the American Humane Association, February, 1976.

Derdeyn, A. Child abuse and neglect: the rights of parents and the needs of their children. *American Journal of Orthopsychiatry*, 1977, 47, 377-385.

Fass, B. *A comparison of high achieving college students with high and low degrees of compulsivity.* Unpublished doctoral dissertation, California School of Professional Psychology, Los Angeles, 1976.

Gelles, R. Demythologizing child abuse. *The Family Coordinator,* 1976, 4, 138-141.

Gross, N., Mason, W., and MacEachern, A. *Explorations in role analysis: studies of the school superintendency role.* NY: John Wiley and Sons, INc., 1966.

Helfer, R., and Kempe, C. *The battered child.* Chicago: University of Chicago Press, 1974.

Helfer, R., and Kempe, C. *Child abuse and neglect: the family and the community.* Cambridge, Mass.: Ballinger Publishing Co., 1976.

Howell, J. Personal communication, Janury 1980.

Kline, P. *Experimental manual for Ai3Q: a measure of the obsessional personality or anal character.* Windsor, Berks: N.F. E.R. Publishing Co., Ltd., 1971.

Lane, R. Political personality and electoral choice. *American Political Sciences Review,* 1955, 49, 173-190.

Lenoski, E.F. *Child abuse.* Unpublished paper. University of Southern California, School of Medicine, 1972.

Los Angeles Police Department's position paper on child abuse, 1976.

Martin, H. *The abused child.* Cambridge, Mass.: Ballinger Publishing Co., 1976.

Mounsey, J. Offenses of criminal violence, cruelty and neglect against children in Lanchashire. In A.W. Franklin (Ed.) *Concerning child abuse.* Edinburg, Scotland: Churchill Livingston, 1975.

Newberger, E., and Bourne, R. The medicalization and legalization of child abuse. *American Journal of Orthopsychiatry,* 1978, 48, 593-607.

Nie, N., Hull, H., Jenkins, J., Steinbrenner, K., and Bent, D. *Statistical package for the social sciences.* NY: McGraw-Hill Book Co., 1975.

Paulsen, J. The law and the abused children. In R. Helfer and C. Kempe (Eds.), *The battered child.* Chicago: University of Chicago Press, 1974.

Pitcher, R.A. The police. In C. Kempe and R. Helfer (Eds.), *Helping the battered child and his family.* Philadelphia: J. B. Lippincott Co., 1972.

Preiss, J., and Ehrlich, H. *An examination of role theory: the case of the state police.* Nebraska: Univ. of Nebraska, 1966.

Pruitt, B. Personal communication. April 15, 1980.

Rehfisch, J. A scale for personality rigidity. *Journal of Consulting Psychology,* 1958, 22, 10-15.

Reiser, M. *Practical psychology for police officers.* Springfield, IL: Charles C. Thomas Publisher, 1973.

Renvoize, J. *Children in danger: the causes and prevention of baby battering.* London: Routledge & Kegan Paul, 1974.

Robinson, J., and Shaver, P. *Measures of social psychological attitudes.* Ann Arbor, MI: Institute for Social Research, 1973.

Schulze, R. A shortened version of the Rokeach Dogmatism Scale. *Journal of Psychological Studies*, 1962, 13, 89-97.

Strauss, M., Gelles, R., and Steinmetz, S. *Violence in the family: an assessment of knowlege and research needs.* Paper presented at the meeting of the American Association for the Advancement of Science. Crime: What we need to know. Boston, February 23, 1976.

Younger, E. *Child abuse.* California Dept. of Justice Information Pamphlet No. 8, August 1976.

APPENDICES

APPENDIX A

STATEMENT OF INFORMED CONSENT

This research project involves the study of attitudes of police officers in relation to situations they may encounter in field investigations. Participation requires approximately 45 minutes during which a paper and pencil test will be administered. All results will be coded to insure your anonymity.

At no time will any of the names of the participants be released.

I, _____, hereby consent to participating in the research being conducted by Joy Dan Graves, Psychology Intern, Behavioral Science Services, Los Angeles Police Department.

I understand that my signature protects my right to total confidentiality.

APPENDIX B

QUESTIONNAIRE

INSTRUCTIONS:

Part Two of the questionnaire is designed to see what attitudes you have about certain areas. There are no right or wrong answers because everyone has the right to his own views. You are asked not to spend time pondering, but to give the first natural answer as it comes to you. The responses are: "strongly agree," "agree," "disagree," and "strongly disagree."

	STRONGLY AGREE	AGREE	DISAGREE	STRONGLY DISAGREE

EXAMPLE:

1. *Money cannot bring happiness.*
If you strongly agree with the above statement you would check the box

	STRONGLY AGREE	AGREE	DISAGREE	STRONGLY DISAGREE
	x			

If you agree with the statement but do not feel strongly about it you would check the box

	STRONGLY AGREE	AGREE	DISAGREE	STRONGLY DISAGREE
		x		

If you disagree with the statement but do not strongly disagree with it you would check the box

	STRONGLY AGREE	AGREE	DISAGREE	STRONGLY DISAGREE
			x	

If you strongly disagree with the above statement you would check the box

	STRONGLY AGREE	AGREE	DISAGREE	STRONGLY DISAGREE
				x

Answer as honestly as possible what is true of you. Do not merely mark what seems the right thing to say to impress the examiner.

QUESTIONNAIRE

1. I feel that what young people need most of all is strict discipline by their parents.
2. I feel most people who don't get ahead just don't have enough willpower.

	STRONGLY AGREE	AGREE	DISAGREE	STRONGLY DISAGREE
3. I feel that a few strong leaders could make this country better than all the laws and talk.				
4. An insult to my honor should not be forgotten.				
5. Parents who abuse their children were often abused as children.				
6. I usually don't like to talk much unless I am with people I know very well.				
7. I must admit that it makes me angry when other people interfere with my daily activity.				
8. I am very slow in making up my mind.				
9. Children two years of age and younger should never be corporally punished.				
10. I must admit I try to see what others think before I take a stand.				
11. Letting my friends down is not so bad because I can't do good all the time for everybody.				
12. I am a better talker than listener.				
13. Neglect is more damaging than physical abuse.				
14. It is my duty to do my job the very best I can.				

	STRONGLY AGREE	AGREE	DISAGREE	STRONGLY DISAGREE
15. Corporal punishment is necessary in order to maintain order.				
16. I would be a lot better off if I could live far away from other people and never have to do anything with them.				
17. I like to talk before groups of people.				
18. Your primary role as a police officer responding to a child abuse complaint is protection of the child.				
19. I make lists of things to do.				
20. I keep a calendar of appointments.				
21. I keep my paper money facing in the same direction.				
22. I don't like to undertake any project unless I have a pretty good idea as to how it will turn out.				
23. At times I feel that I can make up my mind with unusually great ease.				
24. There are two kinds of people in this world; those who are for the truth and those who are against the truth.				
25. Sexual abuse of children is worse than physical abuse.				
26. I try to figure out the shortest or quickest route from one place to another in advance and then follow it.				

	STRONGLY AGREE	AGREE	DISAGREE	STRONGLY DISAGREE
27. Child abuse in the city is increasing.				
28. It is hard for me to start a conversation with strangers.				
29. Substance abuse parents are more likely to abuse their children than non-substance abusers.				
30. I have witnessed a brother, sister or cousin of mine being abused by their parents.				
31. I find that a well-ordered style of life with regular hours is congenial to my temperament.				
32. In this complicated world the only way I can know what's going on is to rely on leaders or experts who can be trusted.				
33. Children just don't know what's good for them				
34. Our country would be better off with fewer elections so I would not have to vote so often.				
35. The trouble with psychology and sociology is that they are not related to the everyday realities of my job as a police officer.				
36. I would like to be an actor on the stage or in the movies.				

	STRONGLY AGREE	AGREE	DISAGREE	STRONGLY DISAGREE
37. The punishment I received as a child was very harsh.				
38. Present training in child abuse investigation is inadequate.				
39. When I start a task, I feel that I must finish it no matter how long it takes.				
40. It bothers me when something unexpected interrupts my daily routine.				
41. My blood boils whenever a person stubbornly refuses to admit he's wrong.				
42. During the course of disciplining children bruises are inevitable.				
43. Police officers should be required to complete certain college courses related to families				
44. I feel the best officers are those who do as they are told by their supervisors.				
45. It is hard for me to act natural when I am with new people.				
46. I find it hard to set aside a task that I have undertaken, even for a short time.				
47. Of all the different philosophies which exist in this world, I believe there is probably only one which is correct.				
48. It is no use worrying about current events or public affairs; I can't do anything about them anyway.				

	STRONGLY AGREE	AGREE	DISAGREE	STRONGLY DISAGREE

49. Affluent people physically abuse their children less than poor people.

50. I try to remember good stories to pass them on to other people.

51. If I have an important appointment I worry about getting there on time.

52. I can be trusted to look out for the needs of the poor as well as the wealthy.

53. I feel nervous if I have to meet a lot of people.

54. The physical punishment children in my family receive is very harsh.

55. I don't like things to be uncertain and unpredictable.

56. It is more important to arrest the parent in a child abuse case than to remove the child.

57. The highest form of government is a democracy and the highest form of democracy is a government run by those who are most intelligent.

58. I should give some of my time for the good of my town or country.

59. When I work on a committee I like to take charge of things.

60. A person who assaults a child should be handled differently than one who

	STRONGLY AGREE	AGREE	DISAGREE	STRONGLY DISAGREE
assaults an adult.				
61. I usually feel nervous and ill-at-ease at a formal dance or party.				
62. The main thing in life is for me to want to do something important.				
63. When I am personally insulted, it affects my work.				
64. The best officers generally have more education than the others.				
65. I just don't give a damn for others.				
66. Harsh physical discipline is that which requires hospitalization.				
67. I know where everything in my room is.				
68. When at an orchestra concert I count the instruments.				
69. At school I usually volunteered for special projects.				
70. The best form of discipline is physical punishment.				
71. I feel very bad when I have failed to finish a job I promised I would do.				
72. I am embarrassed with people I do not know well.				
73. Misdemeanor child abuse is as bad as felony child abuse.				
74. I usually take an active part in the entertainment at parties.				

	STRONGLY AGREE	AGREE	DISAGREE	STRONGLY DISAGREE
75. I'd like it if I could find someone who would tell me how to solve my personal problems.				
76. I find child abuse investigations difficult.				
77. The public has a right to pass judgment on the way the police handle child abuse cases.				
78. Physical abuse of children is worse than sexual abuse.				
79. Most of the ideas which get printed nowadays aren't worth the paper they are printed on.				
80. If there is no trashbasket handy, I drop papers on the ground.				
81. I don't show my emotions and feelings.				
82. It is only when I devote myself to an idea or cause that life becomes meaningful.				
83. As a police officer I have the right to take any action necessary to enforce child abuse laws.				
84. I don't really enjoy most of the work that I do, but I feel that I must do it in order to have the other things that I need and want.				
85. It is often desirable for me to reserve judgment about what's going on until I have had a chance to hear the opinions				

		STRONGLY AGREE	AGREE	DISAGREE	STRONGLY DISAGREE
	of those I respect.				
86.	The present is all too often full of un-happiness. It is only the future that counts.				
87.	Man on his own is a helpless and miser-able creature.				
88.	I keep out of trouble at all costs.				
89.	Corporal punishment is the most effec-tive method of disciplining children.				
90.	Most parents are very cooperative in the investigation of child abuse cases.				
91.	I feel hurt when someone implies that I have not been honest.				
92.	It is easier for me to accept physical abuse of children than it is for me to accept sexual abuse of children.				
93.	I set deadlines for myself when working on a project.				
94.	Please complete this sentence: Child abuse investigations_____				
95.	Feel free to make comments on the back of the question-naire.				
96.	I did not like questions_____				
97.	I liked questions_____ -				

Thank you for participating in this research.

APPENDIX C

INSTRUCTIONS FOR QUESTIONNAIRE

WHAT TO DO:
This questionnaire has two (2) parts to it. The first part is personal data about you. The second part is designed to see what attitudes you have about certain areas.

Try to answer every question. All the information is confidential and will not be disclosed to anyone.

In order for the Behavioral Science Services Section to conduct a follow-up study in the next few years, it is necessary to have some coding that is easily remembered by you. I would like you to code the information either with your social security number, your G.I. number, your driver's license number, or your grandmother's name, as well as you age at the time you completed the question-naire. This number/name will only be known to you. Please write it down someplace where you will remember it.

Remember, *ALL THE INFORMATION OBTAINED WILL BE STRICTLY CONFIDENTIAL.*

Thank you for your cooperation in this research project.

JOY DAN GRAVES, M.S.
Psychology Intern
Behavioral Science Services

MARTIN REISER, Ed.D., Diplomate
in Clinical Psychology, ABPP
Director, Behavioral Science Services

APPENDIX D

QUESTIONNAIRE 2 FOR INTERVIEW SCHEDULE

Basic Information Regarding Officers:

Officer_____

    Age:_____   Sex:_____   Race:_____

    Marital Status:_____   Number of Children:_____

    Age of Children:_____   Sex of Children:_____

    Length of time with department:_____

    Educational Level:_____

    Rank:_____

Special Schools Attended:

_____

_____

_____

_____

Reason for choosing this area of work? (J-car)

_____

_____

_____

_____

Perceived attitude of other officers:

_____

_____

_____

8.   Type of Interaction: (police officer 1)

_____1.   Supportive

_____2.   Threatening

_____3.   Information giving

_____4.   Investigative

_____5.   Other

9.   Type of Interaction: (police officer 2)

_____1.   Supportive

_____2.   Threatening

_____3.   Information giving

_____4.   Investigative

_____5.   Other

10.   Quality of Interaction: (police officer 1)

0	1	2	3	4	5	6	7	8	9	10

Poor   Excellent

11.   Quality of Interaction: (police officer 2)

0	1	2	3	4	5	6	7	8	9	10

Poor   Excellent

12.   Type of Decision:

_____1.   Removal of child

_____2.   Arrest parents

_____3.   Leave child in home and require counseling

_____4.   Admonish parents

_____5.   Removal of siblings from home

_____6.   Follow-up supervision by police officers

_____7.   Other_____

13.   Decision Making Criteria:

_____10   Criminal Justice Code

_____20   Cultural Context

_____30   Personal Judgment

_____31   Appearance

110

_____32   SES Level

_____33   Other_____

14.   Police Officer's Approach:

/_____/

rigid   flexible

/_____/

objective   subjective

15.   Role taken by Officer 1:

_____1.   Adversary

_____2.   Facilitator

16.   Role taken by Officer 2:

_____1.   Adversary

_____2.   Facilitator

17.   How soon did the police call occur after the event?

_____1.   Less than 30 minutes

_____2.   30 minutes - 1 hour

_____3.   1 - 4 hours

_____4.   4 - 24 hours

_____5.   More than 24 hours

(If more than 24 hours, when?)_____

18.   Has abuse occurred before?

_____1.   Yes

_____2.   No

19.   Has any member of the family observed other abuse?

_____1.   Yes (if yes, answer 19a)

_____2.   No

19a.   Which member of the family?

_____1.   Mother

_____2.   Siblings

_____3.   Father

_____4.   Others   (please   explain)_____

20.   Is this a violent family?

_____1.   Yes

_____2.   No

21.   Major area of interaction of abused child:

_____1.   Police officer 1

_____2.   Police officer 2

_____ 3. Participant/observer

_____ 4. Abusing parent

_____ 5. Non-abusing parent

_____ 6. Siblings

_____ 7. Other

Quality of Interaction

/_____/

0   1   2   3   4   5   6   7   8   9   10

22. Major areas of interaction of abusing parent:

_____ 1. Police officer 1

_____ 2. Police officer 2

_____ 3. Participant/observer

_____ 4. Abusing parent

_____ 5. Non-abusing parent

_____ 6. Siblings

_____ 7. Other

Quality of Interaction

/_____/

0   1   2   3   4   5   6   7   8   9   10

23. Major area of interaction of non-abusing parent:

_____ 1. Police officer 1

_____ 2. Police officer 2

_____ 3. Participant/observer

_____ 4. Abusing parent

_____ 5. Non-abusing parent

_____ 6. Siblings

_____ 7. Other

Quality of Interaction

/_____/

0   1   2   3   4   5   6   7   8   9   10

24. Major area of interaction of siblings:

_____ 1. Police officer 1

_____ 2. Police officer 2

_____ 3. Participant/observer

_____ 4. Abusing parent

_____ 5. Non-abusing parent

_____ 6. Siblings

112

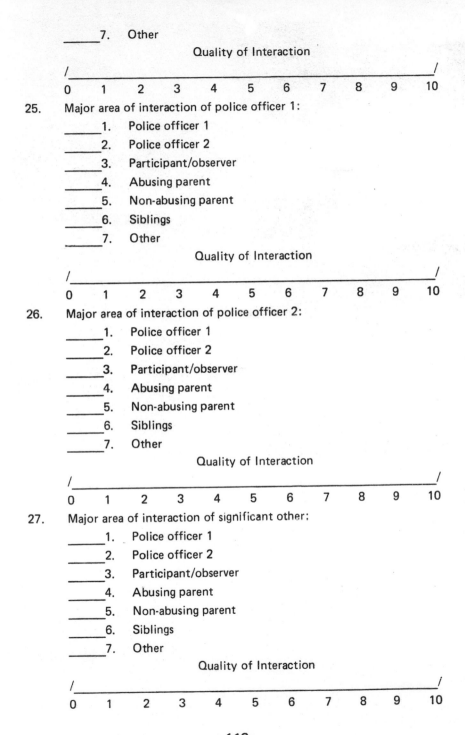

_____ 7. Other

Quality of Interaction

/_____/
0   1   2   3   4   5   6   7   8   9   10

25. Major area of interaction of police officer 1:

_____ 1. Police officer 1

_____ 2. Police officer 2

_____ 3. Participant/observer

_____ 4. Abusing parent

_____ 5. Non-abusing parent

_____ 6. Siblings

_____ 7. Other

Quality of Interaction

/_____/
0   1   2   3   4   5   6   7   8   9   10

26. Major area of interaction of police officer 2:

_____ 1. Police officer 1

_____ 2. Police officer 2

_____ 3. Participant/observer

_____ 4. Abusing parent

_____ 5. Non-abusing parent

_____ 6. Siblings

_____ 7. Other

Quality of Interaction

/_____/
0   1   2   3   4   5   6   7   8   9   10

27. Major area of interaction of significant other:

_____ 1. Police officer 1

_____ 2. Police officer 2

_____ 3. Participant/observer

_____ 4. Abusing parent

_____ 5. Non-abusing parent

_____ 6. Siblings

_____ 7. Other

Quality of Interaction

/_____/
0   1   2   3   4   5   6   7   8   9   10

28. Major area of interaction of reporting party:

_____1. Police officer 1

_____2. Police officer 2

_____3. Participant/observer

_____4. Abusing parent

_____5. Non-abusing parent

_____6. Siblings

_____7. Other

Quality of Interaction

/_____/
0   1   2   3   4   5   6   7   8   9   10

29. Who reported the child abuse?

_____1. School

_____2. Family

_____3. Medical

_____4. Social worker

_____5. Neighbor

_____6. Other

30. Type of abuse:

_____1. Physical

_____2. Sexual

_____3. Injury

_____4. Death

_____5. Neglect

31. Was the abusing parent abused as a child?

_____1. Yes

_____2. No

32. Was the non-abusing parent abused as a child?

_____1. Yes

_____2. No

33. Is the non-abusing parent a colluding parent?

_____1. Yes

_____2. No

_____3. Don't know

34. Who is the abusing party?

_____1. Biological father

_____2. Biological mother

114

_____3. Step parent

_____4. Live-in partner

_____5. Other (please explain)_____

APPENDIX E

QUESTIONNAIRE USED WITH GARDEN GROVE POLICE DEPARTMENT PILOT STUDY

QUESTIONNAIRE

1. Age: Less than 22_____   23 to 34_____   35 to 49_____
   50 or over_____

2. Sex: Male_____   Female_____

3. Marital Status: Single_____   Married_____   Separated_____
   Divorced_____   Divorced and Remarried_____

4. Number of Children: 1 to 2_____   3 to 4_____
   5 to 10_____   10 or more_____

5. Total years of police experience: Less than 5_____   5 to 10_____
   10 or more_____

6. Circle the number or check the space that represents the highest
   number of years of school you have completed.
   _____High School: 1   2   3   4
   _____High School Equivalency Diploma
   _____College: 1   2   3   4
   _____Graduate School: 1   2   3   4   or more
   Major:_____

7. Circle the number that represents the highest number of years of
   school completed by both your mother and father (or guardians).

117

	Father	Mother

Secondary

School 1 2 3 4 5 6 7 8 9 10 11 12   1 2 3 4 5 6 7 8 9 10 11 12

Post Secondary

School 1   2   3   4   1   2   3   4

(e.g., Technical, trade,

business or commercial)

College   1   2   3   4   1   2   3   4

Graduate School 1   2   3   4   1   2   3   4

8.   What is your father's occupation?_____

9.   What is your mother's occupation?_____

10.   What method of punishment did you primarily receive as a child?

_____1. Corporal   _____2. Withdrawal of privileges

_____3. Yelling   _____4. Talking to   _____5. Other

(explain)_____

11.   What method of punishment do the children in your family primarily receive?

_____1. Corporal   _____2. Withdrawal of privileges

_____3. Yelling   _____4. Talking to   _____5. Other

(explain)_____

12.   Are you currently enrolled in college courses related to child growth and development or family psychology?

_____Yes   _____No

APPENDIX F

RIGIDITY SCALE*
(Rehfisch, 1958)

6. I usually don't like to talk much unless I am with people I know very well.
7. I must admit that it makes me angry when other people interfere with my daily activity.
8. I am very slow in making up my mind.
10. I must admit I try to see what others think before I take a stand.
12. I am a better talker than listener.
17. I like to talk before groups of people.
22. I don't like to undertake any project unless I have a pretty good idea as to how it will turn out.
23. At times I feel that I can make up my mind with unusually great ease.
28. It is hard for me to start a conversation with strangers.
31. I find that a well-ordered style of life with regular hours is congenial to my temperament.
36. I would like to be an actor on the stage or in the movies.
40. It bothers me when something unexpected interrupts my daily routine.
45. It is hard for me to act natural when I am with new people.

46. I find it hard to set aside a task that I have undertaken, even for a short time.
59. When I work on a committee, I like to take charge of things.
50. I try to remember good stories to pass them on to other people.
55. I don't like things to be uncertain and unpredictable.
72. I am embarrassed with people I do not know well.
74. I usually take an active part in the entertainment at parties.
81. I don't show my emotions and feelings.
88. I keep out of trouble at all costs.

*Items were modified to be answered in first person and responses were changed.

APPENDIX G

SOCIAL RESPONSIBILITY SCALES
(Berkowitz and Lutterman, 1968)

Social Responsibility Scales*

11. Letting my friends down is not so bad because I can't do good all the time for everybody.
14. It is my duty to do my job the very best I can.
16. I would be a lot better off if I could live far away from other people and never had to do anything with them.
34. Our country would be better off with fewer elections so I would not have to vote so often.
58. I should give some of my time for the good of my town or country.
69. At school I usually volunteered for special projects.
71. I feel very bad when I have failed to finish a job I promised I would do.
48. It is no use worrying about current events or public affairs; I can't do anything about them anyway.
69. At school I usually volunteered for special projects.
71. I feel very bad when I have failed to finish a job I promised I would do.

*Items were modified to be answered in first person and responses were changed.

APPENDIX H

FOUR ITEM F-SCALE
(Schulze, 1962)

Four Item F-Scale*

1. I feel that what young people need most of all is strict discipline by their parents.

2. I feel most people who don't get ahead just don't have enough willpower.

3. I feel that a few strong leaders could make this country better than all the laws and talk.

4. An insult to my honor should not be forgotten.

*Items were modified to first person.

APPENDIX I

SHORT DOGMATISM SCALES*
(Lane, 1955)

24. There are two kinds of people in this world; those who are for the truth and those who are against the truth.
32. In this complicated world of ours the only way we can know what's going on is to rely on leaders or experts who can be trusted.
41. My blood boils whenever a person stubbornly refuses to admit he's wrong.
47. Of all the different philosophies which exist in this world, there is probably only one which is correct.
57. The highest form of government is a democracy, and the highest form of democracy is a governmebt run by those who are most intelligent.
62. The main thing in life is for a person to want to do something important.
79. Most of the ideas which get printed nowadays aren't worth the paper they are printed on.
82. It is only when I devote myself to an idea or cause that life becomes meaningful.
85. It is often desirable for me to reserve judgment about what's going on until I had had a chance to hear the opinions of those I respect.

86. The present is all too often full of unhappiness. It is only the future that counts.
87. Man on his own is a helpless and miserable creature.

*Items were modified to be answered in first person.

37. The punishment I received as a child was very harsh.
54. The physical punishment children in my family receive is very harsh.

(4) = Role of Police Officer

18. Your primary role as a police officer responding to a child abuse complaint is protection of the child.
38. Present training in child abuse investigation is inadequate.
43. Police officers should be required to complete certain college courses related to families.
56. It is more important to arrest the parent in a child abuse case than to remove the child.
60. A person who assaults a child should be handled differently than one who assaults an adult.
76. I find child abuse investigations difficult.
83. As a police officer, I have the right to take any action necessary to enforce child abuse laws.

(5) = General Information

13. Neglect is more damaging than physical abuse.
15. Corporal punishment is necessary in order to maintain order
27. Child abuse in the city is increasing.
33. Children just don't know what's good for them.
42. During the course of disciplining children, bruises are inevitable.
77. The public has a right to pass judgment on the way the police handle child abuse cases.
66. Harsh physical discipline is that which requires hospitalization.
70. The best form of discipline is physical punishment.
73. Misdemeanor child abuse is as bad as felony child abuse.
89. Corporal punishment is the most effective method of disciplining children.
94. Please complete this sentence: Child abuse investigations

_____

_____

_____

APPENDIX K

FOLLOW-UP QUESTIONNAIRE FOR CASE STUDIES

1. Has there been any further abuse reported?
2. What methods of support have been instituted?
3. Is a follow-up being done?
4. By whom?
5. Does the abuser remain in the family home?
6. If no, where is the abuser?
7. Is the abused child in the home?
8. Are the siblings in the home?
9. Other comments.

APPENDIX L

CSB-1 QUESTIONNAIRE*
(Fass and Zelen, 1976)

19. I make lists of things to do.
20. I keep a calendar of appointments.
21. I keep my paper money facing in the same direction.
26. I try to figure out the shortest and quickest route from one place to another in advance and then follow it.
39. When I start a task, I feel that I must finish it no matter how long it takes.
51. If I have an important appointment, I worry about getting there on time.
53. I feel nervous if I have to meet a lot of people.
67. I know where everything in my room is.
68. When at an orchestra concert, I count the instruments.
80. If there is no trashbasket handy, I drop papers on the ground.
91. I feel hurt when someone implies that I have not been honest.
93. I set deadlines for myself when working on a project.

*Items were modified to be answered in first person, and responses were changed from Yes, No to Strongly Agree, Agree, Disagree, and Strongly Disagree.